The
BIBLE
Among the
MYTHS

I asked the earth; and it answered, "I am not He," and whatsoever are therein made the same confession. I asked the sea and the deeps, and the creeping things that lived, and they replied, "We are not thy God, seek higher than we." I asked the breezy air, and the universal air with its inhabitants answered, "Anaximenes was deceived, I am not God." I asked the heavens, the sun, moon and stars. "Neither, say they, "are we the God whom thou seekest." And I answered unto all these things which stand about the door of my flesh, "Ye have told me concerning my God, that ye are not He; tell me something about Him." And with a loud voice they exclaimed, "He made us." My questioning was my observing of them; and their beauty was their reply.... I asked the vast bulk of the earth of my God, and it answered me, "I am not He, but He made me."

— St. Augustine, Confessions 10.6.9

Unique Revelation *or Just* Ancient Literature?

THE
BIBLE
AMONG THE
MYTHS

JOHN N. OSWALT

ZONDERVAN®

ZONDERVAN.com/
AUTHORTRACKER
follow your favorite authors

ZONDERVAN

The Bible among the Myths
Copyright © 2009 by John N. Oswalt

This title is also available as a Zondervan ebook.
Visit www.zondervan.com/ebooks.

Requests for information should be addressed to:

Zondervan, *Grand Rapids, Michigan* 49530

Library of Congress Cataloging-in-Publication Data

Oswalt, John N.
    The Bible among the myths: unique or just different? / John N. Oswalt.
       p. cm.
    Includes bibliographical references and index.
    ISBN 978-0-310-28509-0 (softcover)
    1. Myth in the Old Testament. 2. Bible. O.T. — Historiography. 3. Bible. O.T. — Evidences,
authority, etc. I. Title.
    BS1183.O85   2009
    220.1 — dc22   2008044722

Interior design by Sherri L. Hoffman

Printed in the United States of America

HB 10.31.2023

This book is dedicated to
Dr. Dennis F. Kinlaw
Teacher, Mentor, Confessor, Friend

CONTENTS

Acknowledgments

Along with my teachers, G. Herbert Livingston, Dennis F. Kinlaw, and Cyrus H. Gordon, I also want to express my thanks to several hundred students who have studied this material with me over the past thirty years. They have continually forced me to sharpen and redefine my thinking on the subject.

More recently, I am grateful to colleagues G. Stephen Blakemore, Daniel Block, Tremper Longman III, John Walton, and Joseph Wang, who have read part or all of the manuscript and have made helpful comments. Of course, any errors or inadequacies are my responsibility alone.

To this list I must also add the names of Stanley Gundry, Katya Covrett, and Verlyn Verbrugge, publisher and editors at Zondervan, who have encouraged me and helped to shape the present volume.

Finally, I can only say to Karen, my wife of more years than either of us can believe, without you none of this would be.

INTRODUCTION

The ideas presented in this book have had a long period of maturation. I was first introduced to the subject and the issues in a course entitled "The Literature of the Ancient Near East," taught by Dennis Kinlaw at Asbury Theological Seminary in the 1960s. The seeds planted there began to germinate and grow during my graduate study with Cyrus Gordon in the Mediterranean Studies department at Brandeis University. They have reached their present level of maturity (such as that is) as a result of thinking them through with students in courses I have taught at Asbury Theological Seminary, Trinity Evangelical Divinity School, and Wesley Biblical Seminary.

In the period of time since that first course at Asbury Theological Seminary, thinking on the subject has undergone an almost complete change of direction. By the late 1940s two world wars punctuated by a world-wide economic depression had raised some serious questions about the evolutionary paradigm inherent in the philosophy of Idealism. And since that paradigm was all but inseparable from the standard higher critical views of the Old Testament that had prevailed for the previous fifty years, there was cause for some rethinking about the Old Testament and the religion it promulgated.

That rethinking was led by William F. Albright and his students, among them G. Ernest Wright of the Harvard Divinity School. Speaking for much of the scholarly community of the time, Wright argued that the differences between the Israelite way of thinking about reality and the way in which Israel's neighbors approached that topic were so significant that no evolutionary explanations could account for them.[1] But now, nearly sixty years later, it is widely affirmed that Israelite religion is simply one more of the complex of West Semitic religions, and that its characteristic features can be fully explained on the basis of evolutionary change.[2]

---

1. G. Ernest Wright, *The Old Testament against Its Environment* (London: SCM, 1950).
2. See, e.g., Mark Smith, *The Origins of Biblical Monotheism* (Oxford: Oxford Univ. Press, 2001).

What has happened to cause such a dramatic change in thinking? Have some new discoveries made Wright's position untenable? No, they have not. The literatures of the ancient Near East, including that of Ugarit, which are now cited to prove the case against Wright, were already widely known at the time his book was written. The Dead Sea Scrolls were just coming to light, but they have not materially altered the picture of ancient Israel that was known in 1950. So what is the explanation? I do not wish to belittle either the ability or the motivation of current scholars. Their mastery of the field and their genuine concern to ferret out "the real facts" are not in question. Nonetheless, I am convinced that it is prior theological and philosophical convictions that account for the change and not any change in the data.

In 1950, largely because of the work of Karl Barth, the scholarly world was ready to entertain the idea of revelation in ways it had not been for at least a couple of generations. Undoubtedly, the near destruction of European civilization in the previous forty years contributed to that readiness. Revelation assumes that this world is not self-explanatory and that some communication from beyond it is necessary to explain it. Ready to believe in such a possibility, Old Testament scholars in the 1950s saw evidence for it in the manifest differences between the understandings found in the Old Testament and the understandings of all the peoples around Israel. None of that data has changed. The differences between Genesis and the Babylonian account of the origins of the world, for example, are unmistakable to anyone who reads them side by side.

But the idea that this world is not self-explanatory and that revelation from beyond it is necessary to understand it is profoundly distasteful to us humans. It means that we are not in control of our own destiny or able to make our own disposition of things for our own benefit. This thought, the thought that we cannot supply our ultimate needs for ourselves, that we are dependent on someone or something utterly beyond us, is deeply troublesome. This is especially true in the light of the revolution in thinking that occurred in the United States in the 1960s and 1970s. The turn away from outside authority of all sorts to extreme individual autonomy was utterly inimical to the idea of revelation. So, although the biblical and ancient Near Eastern data had not changed at all, the possible way of explaining that data did change. Revelation was no longer an option. But without revelation, how can the differences be explained?

It is at this point that another feature of the Old Testament enters the discussion: the undoubted similarities that exist between the literature and culture of Israel and the literatures and cultures of Israel's neighbors. Modern scholars who cannot admit the possibility of revelation now insist that the differences that were so unmistakable to scholars a generation ago are not really that important at all, but it is the similarities that are vital, showing that Israelite religion is not essentially different from the religions around it.[3] This must be so if Israelite religion is merely one of the evolutionary developments from those religions.

Here we come to the vital philosophical distinction between "essence" and "accident." When we analyze an object, we try to determine which of its characteristics are "essentials" and which are "accidentals."[4] If you remove an essential feature, the thing will cease to be itself; but if you remove an accidental, there will be no change in the object's essential being. So with humanity, hair is an accidental, while self-consciousness is an essential.

But how does this apply to the discussion at hand? What is essential to Israelite religion? Is it the differences between its understandings of life and those found in the religions of its neighbors? Wright and a large number of other scholars of the 1950s would say yes. Remove these characteristics and it would no longer be itself. The many similarities to the religions of Israel's neighbors were "accidentals." So the fact that all of the developed cultures of the ancient Near East worshiped their deity (deities) in temples of similar structure is important, but not essential. What is essential was that there was no idol in the innermost cell of the Jerusalem temple. Today, the situation is turned on its head. Now it is the similarities that are understood to

---

3. It is disingenuous for a modern atheistic scholar to demean the scholarship of Albright because he was supposedly an evangelical (!). Albright would certainly dispute that claim. But even if it were true, are we to think that atheism has no influence on one's scholarship in approaching and understanding literature about God? On this point see Timothy J. Keller, *The Reason for God: Belief in an Age of Skepticism* (New York: Dutton, 2008).

4. In common usage today, an "accident" is a chance happening. But in philosophical vocabulary an "accident" is a feature of an object that is not essential to that object's being. In music, flats and sharps are "accidentals." The note is essentially a G, whether flatted or sharped.

be essentials, while the differences are merely accidentals. What is essential is that Israel worshiped a god, as every other West Semitic religion did. The fact that the Old Testament insists from beginning to end that there is only one being worthy to be called "god" is an accidental.

This issue of differences and similarities will provide the focal point around which this book will revolve. Is the religion of the Old Testament essentially similar to, or essentially different from, the religions of its neighbors? That discussion will be further focused in two areas: myth and history. Is the Old Testament more like the myths found in its neighboring cultures, or it is something else? Is it one more creation of humans trying to encapsulate the divine, or is it the miraculously preserved account of the one God, Yahweh, disclosing himself in unique events, persons, and experiences in time and space? In this regard we will look carefully at the vexed problem of the definition of "myth." I will attempt to show that if "myth" is defined in terms of its common characteristics and functions, the Bible, whatever it is, does not accord with that definition.

Along the way in this discussion, I will point out that once a person or a culture adopts the idea that this world is all there is, as is typical of myth, certain things follow regardless of the primitiveness or the modernity of the person or culture. Among these are the devaluing of individual persons, the loss of an interest in history, fascination with magic and the occult, and denial of individual responsibility. The opposites of these, among which are what we have taken to be the glories of modern Western culture, are the by-products of the biblical worldview. As that worldview is progressively lost among us, we are losing the by-products as well. Not realizing that they are by-products, we are surprised to see them go, but we have no real explanation for their departure.

As I said above, one striking difference between the Old Testament and the literatures of the ancient Near East that emerges from a comparative study of the two is the medium by which the divine is known. Among Israel's neighbors (and indeed, everywhere else in the world) the medium is nature.[5] But in Israel nature is only a distant second (see, e.g., Ps 19 or

---

5. This is not to say that the gods of Israel's neighbors never were thought to act in human-historical experiences. They certainly were thought to do so. But this was not the primary and consistent medium through which they were to be known, as was the case with Israel's God.

Isa 6:3). Far and away, the medium in Israel is unique human-historical experience.

But that recognition raises a further question that will provide the second pole of our study. Are we to think that the experiences described in the Old Testament actually took place? And is it necessary that we think they did? In other words, are these accounts truly historical, and does it matter? For most of the history of the church, that was a meaningless question. Of course these things happened; how could one think otherwise? Compared to the legends and sagas of the world, these narratives breathe authenticity in ways unlike anything else until the attempts of novelists in the last 250 years to give their creations "verisimilitude."[6]

Yet today we find an increasing skepticism about the veracity of the Bible's statements about what took place in the past. It is often said that the accounts found in the Bible are only "history-like." In response, we will look at the characteristics of biblical historical narrative and compare them with the ancient Near Eastern approaches to the past. Once again, we will note that whatever the biblical narratives are, they are in a different category altogether. If they do not conform to all the canons of modern history writing, they are still much closer to what characterizes that genre than they are to anything in the ancient world. I will attempt to explain why that is the case.

But if modern historical criticism is correct, then we cannot accept that most of the events described in Scripture took place as Scripture reports them. What then? Can the theology that is mediated to us through the historical narratives of the Old Testament be extricated from it? In other words, can we still believe in the God of Scripture if the medium through which he is presented to us is demonstrably false? I think not, because the theology of the Bible is presented as though it is an extrapolation from the experience of Israel and the church. The doctrine of election is a result of the historical fact of the Exodus, not the reverse. The land is Israel's because it is a feudal gift from God given to them as they faithfully followed Joshua into the land in the conquest. God is God and the Babylonian gods

---

6. "Verisimilitude" is the attempt to give the aura of reality to a piece of fiction. It would be especially characteristic of modern historical fiction for the writing of which the author has done extensive research into the period being written about.

are nothing because he predicts the future specifically and they cannot. Thus, the New Testament claim that we have eternal life because Jesus Christ walked out of the tomb on the first day of a certain week is not an innovation; it is simply continuing on in the trajectory that was laid out from Genesis to Chronicles (in the Hebrew order of the books). If none of these events actually took place, we are left with two insuperable problems: Where did the theology come from, and where did the Israelites get the idea of rooting their theology in (fictional) human history?

Finally, the veracity of the theological claims of the Old Testament is inseparable from the veracity of the historical claims. I do not wish to set up a simplistic "either-or" argument here. There are important issues that must be addressed. To argue for the veracity of the Old Testament reports is not to close off discussion about the exact nature of those reports. Issues of poetic descriptions versus prose accounts must be taken into consideration. The ways in which an ancient Semite handles data must not be confused with the ways in which an ultra-modern thinker does. The import of the data is open to varying interpretations, and room must be left for such discussion.

But the starting point of the investigation is vital. Do we begin with a bias for the Bible's integrity as a historical witness, confident that when rightly interpreted the data will be self-consistent, and are we willing to suspend judgment when no obvious resolution for discrepancies presents itself? Or do we begin with a bias against that integrity, finding in every problem or discrepancy evidence that demands we either deny the faith or create some means of saving it that will in the end be insupportable? The comment of James Orr from a hundred years ago is still highly apropos:

> Let one assume, and hold fast by the idea, that there has really been a great scheme of historical revelation extending through successive dispensations, and culminating in the Incarnation in Jesus Christ, and many things will appear natural and fitting as parts of such a scheme, which otherwise would be rejected as incredible, or be taken account of only to be explained away.[7]

---

7. James Orr, *The Problem of the Old Testament* (London: Nisbett, 1907), 85. I do not mean to suggest that the only persons who have come to doubt the historical veracity of the Old Testament are those who begin with a bias in that direction. Many honest investigators

Ultimately, the unique worldview of the Old Testament undergirds its claims of historical reliability. When we ask the Israelites where they came up with these fantastic concepts, they tell us they *did not* "come up" with them. They tell us that God broke in upon their lives and dragged them kicking and screaming into these understandings. They tell us that they did their best to get away from him, but that he would not let them go. He kept obtruding himself into their lives in the most uncomfortable ways. If that report is not true, we are at a loss to explain where the fundamentally different understandings of life in the Old Testament came from.

In the end, I am not advocating a "the Bible says it, and I believe it, and that settles it" point of view, although those who disagree with me may argue that to be the case. What I am advocating is a willingness to allow the Bible to determine the starting place of the investigation.

I am not insisting that all historical questions in the Bible can be solved with simplistic answers, or that if a person has questions he or she is necessarily doubting the Bible's revelational authority. I am arguing that the Bible will not allow us to disassociate its historical claims from its theological claims, and that our investigations of the history should not assume that they can be so disassociated. I am not suggesting that we should solve historical or theological discrepancies by forcing strained harmonizations upon them. I am asking that we allow the possibility of harmonization and not begin by assuming that any discrepancy can only be explained by a denial of the Bible's own claims in the matter.

I am far from denying that there are many similarities between Israel and its neighbors, or that an understanding of those similarities is significant for understanding the Israelite people and its experience. The studies of Israel and the ancient Near East in the last 150 years have been immensely valuable in that regard.[8] But I am asking that we not overplay

---

who began with the opposite bias have come to that conclusion. I only mean to say that if we begin with the bias against its veracity, it is virtually certain that we will come to that conclusion. Nor do I mean to say that reaching that conclusion one must necessarily abandon faith. However, it is my observation that such a faith, hanging in the air, as it were, is virtually incapable of reproducing itself. Our students tend to be more logical than we.

8. See most recently John H. Walton, *Ancient Near Eastern Thought and the Old Testament: Introducing the Conceptual World of the Hebrew Bible* (Grand Rapids: Baker Academic, 2006).

those similarities so that they obscure the much more significant differences that affect every interpretation of the similarities. What I *am* calling for in the end is that the evidence supporting the Bible's claims to have been revealed be given the attention that it deserves, and that arguments growing from a fundamental disbelief in that possibility not be given a privileged place in the discussion.

PART 1

THE BIBLE AND MYTH

CHAPTER 1

THE BIBLE IN ITS WORLD

The Western world has been founded on a certain way of looking at reality. Obviously that way of understanding is an amalgam of many separate contributions. But without minimizing the importance of others, it can be asserted with confidence that the Bible is the single most important of these contributors, especially when its outlook was integrated with the contributions of Greek philosophy first by Augustine and then by Thomas Aquinas. These thinkers showed that the transcendent monotheism of the Bible provided the metaphysical foundation for Greek thought, while using Greek thought provided a means of logically organizing the observations about reality found in the biblical narratives.

GREEK THOUGHT

The Greek philosophers of the seventh through the third centuries BC[1] intuited that this is a "universe" and not a "polyverse." They believed that there must be a single unifying principle in the cosmos. Furthermore, they believed that this is a real world in which effects are the result of observable causes. In addition, they believed that these causes and effects were discoverable through rational thought. At the foundation of this thought was the conviction that something could not be so and not so at the same time.[2]

---

1. I am writing as a Christian. Therefore, I will continue to use the conventions of the last two millennia in the West. I refer to the sixty-six books of Christian Scripture as "the Bible," labeling its first thirty-nine books "the Old Testament" and its last twenty-seven books "the New Testament." I refer to the time prior to Christ's birth as BC and the time since that event as AD.

2. For a good summary treatment of the Greek philosophers, see volumes 1 and 2 of *The Columbia History of Western Philosophy*, ed. R. H. Popkin (New York: Columbia Univ. Press, 2005).

Increasingly, this way of thinking brought the Greek philosophers into conflict with the dominant thought of the world up until that time. That thought insisted that this *is* a "polyverse" in which we live, wherein existence is the result of the conflict of many different forces, most of them unseen, and many of them unknowable. As a result, it becomes all but impossible to determine why anything that happens does happen. There are an almost infinite number of potential causes for any event, and the majority of these are in the realm of the invisible, which is the "real" world. Because of the fundamental unreality of the observable world, it is entirely possible for something to be so and not so at the same time.

Ultimately, this conflict between the philosophers and the prevailing religious culture was won by the culture. Socrates was forced to drink hemlock, and while Plato[3] and Aristotle, his successors, were able to live out their lives, they were the end of their line. While the philosophic tradition was never really submerged into Greek thought, it was never able to exercise a dominant hold on the Greek culture. Instead, what dominated the culture was the world of myth, with all of the characteristics just mentioned, which had that hold.

The Greek playwright Euripides, in his play *The Bacchae*, portrays this struggle and its eventual outcome in a devastating way. He uses a group of men to represent the rational side of human nature and depicts them explaining why their point of view is much superior to the largely irrational, but ultimately more vital aspects of that nature represented by a group of women. The action centers upon the annual "Bacchanalia" when Bacchus, god of wine, is celebrated. The men want to reduce this worship to a set of rather lifeless ideas and theorems while the women want to participate in the inexplicable, but terribly real experience of unity with the god. Ultimately the women win, hacking the men to pieces in the course of the worship. It takes little explanation to understand the author's point: rational thought is finally unable to compete with the mysterious and largely inchoate world of affective experience.

There is a certain irony in *The Bacchae* because it was almost the last of the great Greek dramas. These dramas were written to be performed

---

3. In Plato we see a learned attempt to integrate the two ways of thinking with his idea of the invisible forms, of which all visible forms were inadequate reflections.

during the Bacchanalia, and they were an attempt to wrestle with the great issues of life, especially as these were exposed in the conflict between the two ways of looking at life that the Greeks were experiencing during this time. As one of the last of these great dramas, *The Bacchae* seems to be a historical statement admitting that the attempt to integrate the two opposing views had failed and that the old antirational way had won.

HEBREW THOUGHT

At the same time as the Greek philosophers were struggling to articulate their point of view, there was a parallel series of events taking place at the eastern end of the Mediterranean. Between 625 BC and 400 BC the Israelite people went through the crisis of their faith. While Old Testament scholars continue to argue about the precise historical details of this crisis, the general outlines are clear enough. The crisis was prompted by the rise of first the Assyrian and then the Babylonian empires. The ability of these two groups to achieve military and political dominance over large parts of the ancient Near East called Israel's particular faith into question.

This faith had been and continued to be drawn in sharp relief by a series of persons we know as the prophets. The prophets had articulated an understanding of reality that was starkly different from that of the peoples around them. The present editions of what those leaders said assert that these ideas did not originate with the prophets, but the prophets were only trying to call the people back to understandings that had been theirs from the very time of their emergence as a people hundreds of years earlier. Among those ideas were the following: there is only one God; God is the sole Creator of all that is; since this world is not an emanation from him, it has a real existence of its own; God has revealed himself to humans primarily in the context of their unique experiences in space and time; he has communicated an explicit will for human behavior in this world; and he rewards and punishes on the basis of obedience to that will.

Much like the positions of the Greek philosophers, these ideas came into direct conflict with the views that were current all around Israel: there are many gods; the visible world is an emanation from them and as such has no real existence of its own; the gods are known through their identity with the great natural cycles of the cosmos; the gods have no purposes except those that humans have: survival, dominance, comfort, and pleasure; humans exist to provide these for the gods; if humans do care for the gods, the gods will reward them; and if they do not, the gods will punish them.

As a result of this conflict in understandings of reality, the eventual capture of Israel first by the Assyrians and then by the Babylonians caused a real crisis of faith. The Israelites realized that these two different understandings of reality could not coexist. If they had not formally expressed the logic of noncontradiction as the Greek philosophers had, they still understood that if the other understanding of reality was correct, then theirs was false. And surely the fact that the Assyrians and the Babylonians had triumphed over them showed that the Assyrians and Babylonians, and everybody else, were correct. So would the unusual Israelite faith disappear? When Jerusalem finally fell, would the final remnant adhering to that faith in Judah give it all up and admit that they had been wrong?

As a matter of fact they did not! There is no Old Testament version of *The Bacchae*, for the pagan vision of reality did not triumph in Israel. Why it did not is still, and probably will remain, a matter of controversy. As far as the biblical text is concerned, there were several contributing factors. One was the fact that the prophets had boldly predicted that the Assyrian and Babylonian conquests would be evidence of God's work in history to punish his unbelieving people. But coupled with this prediction of that conquest and the exile was also the prediction of the return from exile, something that had never occurred before during the many centuries in which exile had been practiced as an instrument of foreign policy. Thus, when the exile and the return did occur as predicted, it certainly became easier for Israelite believers to believe that the interpretation of the exile that the prophets had given was the correct one: it was not an indication of the triumph of the gods, but of God using the pagan nations as his tools.

Another factor that played a part in the survival of the peculiarly Israelite worldview was, according to the text, the survival of an authoritative collection of books that the Israelites understood to record the origin of their faith and the narrative of the ways in which that faith had fared in the Israelite experience. Thus the priest Ezra returned from Babylon with the authority to teach "the Torah of his God," which was the core of the collection (Ezra 7:25). And one of the early acts of Nehemiah, after the rebuilding of the Jerusalem city walls, was to sponsor a public occasion in which Ezra read that Torah to the people (Neh 8:1 – 3). Thus, in addition to any subjective faith that the people might have had, there was an objective standard that stood over against them and called them to account.

To be sure, it appears that the Israelites swung directly out of one ditch into another. Prior to, and immediately after, the exile, according to the text, there was a tendency to take a rather cavalier attitude toward God's commands. Many people thought they could live according to the pagan worldview while giving lip service to the biblical one. Because of the work of Ezra, Nehemiah, and Malachi, whom we know, and many others whose names we do not know, there came the conviction that the only way to avoid another dose of divine punishment was to get serious about worshiping Yahweh exclusively. Unfortunately, the understanding of exclusive worship that developed was one of literalistic obedience to the commands without the kind of alteration of attitude that the commands were designed to foster. But be that as it may, the survival of the distinctly biblical understanding of reality was assured.

COMBINING GREEK AND HEBREW THOUGHT

What we find, then, at the beginning of the Christian era was, on the one hand, the biblical worldview, which had not been worked out with philosophical consistency, but which had about it a vigor and a vitality stemming from its survival in the crucible of life. On the other hand, there was the worldview of Greek philosophy, which did have the logical consistency but had proven unable to be translated into the common experience. It was when the gospel of Jesus, presupposing the Israelite worldview, penetrated into the Greco-Roman world that the stage was set for the combination of the Greek and the Hebrew worldviews in the distinctively Christian way.

As a result of that combination there was now an explanation for the Greek intuition of a universe: there is one Creator who has given rise to the universe and in whose creative will it finds its unity. At the same time the Greeks showed the Hebrews the logical implications of their monotheism. In the Hebrew idea of sole creatorship by a transcendent Deity there is a basis for the idea that this world is a real one: God has spoken it into existence as an entity separate from himself; it is not merely an emanation of the gods. But the Greeks could show the Hebrews that in this real world there is a linkage of cause and effect that the Hebrews tended to overlook in their emphasis upon the First Cause.

Now there is a basis for the law of noncontradiction in the recognition that God is not the world and the world is not God. There is such a thing as truth because the one Creator of the universe is absolutely reliable and faithful to his Word. The idea that the Creator is primarily known in this world and especially in relation to unique events in human-historical experience provides the basis for the concept of historical responsibility.

To be sure, the full development of this combination was a long time in coming. The platonic cast of much of early Christian thought perhaps did more to hinder it than to help it. It is only with the recovery of Aristotle that resulted from the various interactions with Islam[4] (beginning with the Crusades) that the full implications began to be worked out. Then for the first time logic and science began to be worked out in detail. At last logic and science had an understanding of metaphysical reality under them that was fully consistent with them. At the same time the Christendom of the Dark Ages was called back from the bifurcation between heaven and earth that had sprung up from an essentially magical view of faith.

THE NECESSITY OF THE BIBLICAL WORLDVIEW

One important conclusion that must be drawn from all of this is that contrary to the nineteenth- and twentieth-century delusion, science and logic are not self-evident. They cannot stand on their own. It was not until the biblical idea of one personal, transcendent, purposeful Creator was allowed to undergird them that science and logic were able to be fully developed and to come into their own.[5] Without that undergirding, they fall to the ground

---

4. Aristotelian philosophy was preserved in one form or another in Islamic schools because of Islam's rigid monotheism. Christendom was at first more attracted to Platonic thought with its idea of invisible universal ideals.

5. Stanley L. Jaki, *The Origin of Science and the Science of Its Origin* (South Bend, IN: Regnery/Gateway, 1979).

under a barrage of contrary data, just as Euripides' pale, rationalistic men fell under the knives of the vital, earthy women. We in the last two centuries have shown the truth of this statement. We have tried to make logic and science stand on their own, and they have begun to destroy themselves.

The unique linkage of Greek and Israelite thought led to several characteristic features of Western civilization. Included among these are: the validity of reason, the importance of history, the worth of the individual, and the reality of nature. But in the revolt of the Enlightenment against what it saw as the stultifying strictures of Christian dogma, these and other results were made ultimate values.

What has happened? Rationality has become rationalism. We have made the human mind the measure of all things and the result was a century in which two of the chief accomplishments were Buchenwald and Hiroshima. Rationalism has taught us that there is nothing worth thinking about. History has become historicism, in which we assert that finally we can know nothing about the past except what we make up to serve our own historical fictions. Individuality has become individualism, in which we assert that individual rights come before everything else, with the result that we are each locked in lonely isolation. Nature has become naturalism, in which the cosmos becomes an end in itself serving its own implacable, mindless, and deterministic ends. In many ways Western culture and civilization is playing out *The Bacchae* again. We can no longer answer the "so what" questions. Reason for what? History for what? Individuality for what? Nature for what? In the absence of these answers we fall back to the pursuit of survival, dominance, comfort, and pleasure.

How has this happened? It has happened because the leaders of the Enlightenment thought Greek logic and science could stand on their own. They thought that the biblical understanding of reality was a hindrance that must be cut away so that rationality, history, individual worth, and natural reality could stand forth in their true worth. Surely there was some reason for this attitude. The church of the late eighteenth century, whether Orthodox, Roman Catholic, or Protestant, was an intensely conservative institution intent on preserving itself and on putting down all those who wished to think for themselves. But tragically, the understanding of reality that the Enlightenment thinkers took to be a hindrance was the absolutely necessary underpinning. By stripping it away, they left logic and science defenseless against all the old gods.

In this book I want to examine the distinctive view of reality that is first found in the Old Testament as it presently stands and which provides the underlying assumptions for the New Testament. I will show why current attempts to describe the Bible as one more of the world's great myths are incorrect. I will argue that in the end there are only two worldviews: the biblical one and the other one. I will demonstrate why the Christian faith cannot be other than exclusivist. I will show how current trends in the United States in particular are the logical result of the loss of biblical faith. In passing, I will ask whether any other explanation than the one the Bible claims (direct communication with the one God) can explain where this understanding of reality came from. In the end I hope to have convinced younger readers especially of the necessity of standing absolutely firm on the biblical understanding of reality and of giving no quarter to what is, in the end, the enemy.

CHAPTER 2

THE BIBLE AND MYTH: A PROBLEM OF DEFINITION

A SHIFT IN UNDERSTANDING

The first question we must answer is whether the Bible does indeed have a distinctive view of reality. Fifty years ago there would have been little debate on this issue. Scholars in both Old and New Testament studies would have agreed with Harvard professor G. Ernest Wright when he said "the God of Israel has no mythology."[1] G. Stählin, writing in the *Theological Dictionary of the New Testament*, concluded that "myth" was not a useful category for biblical interpretation.[2]

Likewise, Artur Weiser could say that the monotheism of the Bible and its connection with history do not allow mythmaking.[3] To be sure, none of these writers, or many others who would have agreed with them on this point, would have argued that all the narratives in the Bible were historically accurate. Neither would they have argued that it was impossible for the biblical accounts, especially those in the Old Testament, to have had their origins in some sort of mythical perceptions. They were simply saying that the biblical literature, as it now stands, does not share the dominant characteristics of myth.

Today, however, opinions have radically changed. Robert A. Oden claims that there is a real possibility that mythical thought and mythical

---

1. G. E. Wright, *The Old Testament against Its Environment* (London: SCM, 1950), 26.
2. G. Stählin, "μῦθος," *Theological Dictionary of the New Testament*, ed. G. Kittel, trans. G. Bromiley (Grand Rapids: Eerdmans, 1967), 4:795.
3. A. Weiser, *Introduction to the Old Testament*, trans. D. Barton (London: Darton, Longman and Todd, 1961), 58.

literature are at the very heart of Israel's religion.[4] Almost as direct is the statement of Mark Smith, who says "the Baal cycle expresses the heart of the West Semitic religion from which Israelite religion largely developed."[5] And J. W. Rogerson says that a study of myth may yield "insights that will assist biblical interpretation."[6]

What accounts for such a radical shift? To a significant degree it has to do not with the discovery of new data, but with the shift in the prevailing assumptions of scholars. For the period of time between about 1865 and 1925 the dominant mood of Old Testament scholars was that the Old Testament was simply a child of its times and that Old Testament thought and religion had merely evolved out of the general religious milieu of the ancient Near East. To be sure it was the final and decisive step, leaving its predecessors far behind, but it was still the result of an evolutionary process in which humanity discovered more and more clearly the truth about deity.

But through the 1920s and 1930s there came to be greater and greater dissatisfaction with this description of the facts. Many scholars have pointed to the horrors of World War I as a cause for questioning whether the evolution of thought was necessarily always upward. It began to be argued that new thought unconditioned by its predecessors, that is, revelation, was a real possibility. In the field of systematic theology the Swiss theologian Karl Barth spoke out strongly in favor of the idea that biblical thought could not be explained in evolutionary terms.[7] Thus, in the 1940s, 1950s, and 1960s there appeared a number of works in the biblical fields in which, while influence from the surrounding cultures was not denied, there were strong arguments for the ultimate uniqueness of the biblical religion. The title of Wright's book, *The Old Testament against its Environment*, aptly expresses the mood of these times.

But by the 1960s that mood was already beginning to change. Fundamental to this change was the recognition that there was a contradiction

---

4. Robert Oden, "Myth and Mythology (OT)," *Anchor Bible Dictionary*, ed. D. N. Freedman (Garden City, NY: Doubleday, 1995), 4:960.
5. M. Smith, *The Ugaritic Baal Cycle* (Leiden: Brill, 1994), 1:xxvii.
6. J. W. Rogerson, "Slippery Words: V. Myth," *Expository Times* 110 (1978): 13.
7. So Barth strongly objected to the use of the category of myth in reference to the Bible. See below.

inherent in the thinking of Barth and those who followed him. On the one hand, they stressed strongly the idea that the Bible was unique from all its surrounding cultures in its use of human-historical experience as the locus of revelation. But on the other hand, they admitted the correctness of the prevailing scholarly opinion that the historical records contained in the Bible were largely incorrect. Younger scholars such as James Barr and Brevard Childs pointed out the inconsistency in this thinking. If the historical basis on which the supposed revelation rested was false, then why should we give any special credence to the ideas resting on that basis?

Thus began a sweeping shift away from any idea that biblical thought was unique either in its origins or in its ultimate formulations. So if it was appropriate to describe other religious systems as *myth*, there could be no reason to exclude the biblical religion from that terminology. It must be said that there have been no major new discoveries either in the realm of myth or in the ancient Near East that have caused this shift. To be sure, there continues to be an appeal to the ancient Near Eastern data we have, and there has been a great broadening of the definition of the term *myth* to make it possible to include the Bible in the category, but it is a change of assumptions that accounts for the shift, not new discoveries.

IS IT APPROPRIATE TO CLASSIFY THE BIBLE AS MYTH?

How can we adjudicate this difference of opinion? Is it appropriate to call the Bible myth or not? Surely that depends on the definition of the term *myth*. Furthermore, it is important to understand why there is such a desire at the present time to force the Bible into that category. Oden says that the "assumption that all things biblical must be forever distinguished from the nonbiblical and, especially, the mythological world" is the only basis "for the otherwise inexplicable desire to divide the OT from myth."[8] However, we might ask Oden the contrary question, "Whence comes the great desire to break down that division?" In fact, it may be argued that the broadening of the definition that has occurred in recent years has been precisely in order to facilitate the breaking down of the division.

---

8. Oden, "Myth and Mythology (OT)," 4:960.

The Problem of Definition

This brings us to one of the thorniest problems in this entire undertaking. What is a myth? Rogerson goes so far as to say that there are so many differences of opinion on the subject that no one definition is possible.[9] But if that is true, then no more discussion is possible. Each person will define the term as he or she wishes, and no basis for meaningful conversation remains. This sounds much like a situation where the rules of logic no longer exist, a world in which the single standards of either the Bible or Greek logic have been dispensed with.

But that is a counsel of despair that we need not follow. We can at least make a case that "myth" is A and not B on the basis of the evidence. We may be charged with misuse of the evidence or with overlooking some important piece of evidence or with some other logical fault, but we will not agree that a word can mean whatever someone chooses to make it mean.

When we evaluate the validity of a definition, we must first ask whether it is broad enough to include all the items that manifestly share the majority of the common characteristics of the class being defined. Then we must ask whether the definition is narrow enough to exclude those items that only exhibit one or two of the common characteristics. This is a major problem with the definitions of myth. Given the recent desire to break down any distinction between the Bible and the mythological, there has been a marked broadening of definitions. It is as though we have defined an automobile as "a vehicle having wheels." As far as it goes the definition is accurate: automobiles are vehicles with wheels. But it is not a helpful definition because it will include a lot of things that are clearly not automobiles, like wheelbarrows. If, however, we were to define automobiles as "self-propelled, gasoline-powered, four-wheeled passenger vehicles," the definition would be too narrow because there are some automobiles that are powered with diesel fuel, and some that have but three wheels.

A second definitional problem has to do with the very nature of the definition. Does the definition describe the items in the class or does it evaluate them? If we say that a legend is a false story about the past while a history is a true account of the past, we involve ourselves in the question, "false or true

---

9. Rogerson, "Slippery Words," 13.

according to what standard?" The definition includes an evaluation that may or may not be helpful in defining the members of the class. As we will see, this has been a continuing problem in the definition of myth.

Historical-Philosophical Definitions

For our purposes, we may group the definitions under two main headings according to their type. They are the historical-philosophical and the phenomenological, or descriptive.[10] We may further subdivide the historical-philosophical definitions into three groups: the etymological, the sociological, and the literary. As the overall heading suggests, these latter three definitions all have in common the offering of a critical evaluation of the material they are describing. As mentioned above, the danger here is that the critical evaluation may import something into the definition that is in fact not inherent in the thing being defined.

Etymological Definitions

Etymological definitions of myth stress the falsity of the thing being described. This derives from the meaning of the Greek word *mythos*. The Greeks used the word to describe "a false legend of the gods."[11] It was a story that all the evidence showed did not take place. Thus we have such a typical dictionary definition as "a purely fictitious narrative usually involving supernatural persons, actions, or events and embodying some popular idea concerning natural or historical phenomena."[12] This is, of course, the definition known by the person on the street. If someone speaks to them of the "myth of George Washington throwing a half-dollar across the Potomac" or the "myth of the resurrection," they understand the speaker primarily to be making a judgment about the historical veracity of those reports. To call the Bible a myth in this sense is to say that its attempts to express the nature of reality, like those of the other ancient Near Eastern religions, are rooted in falsehood.

---

10. I am indebted to B. Childs for this division and terminology. The discussion may be found in his *Myth and Reality in the Old Testament* (London: SCM, 1960), 13 – 16.
11. See the discussion by Stählin, "μῦθος," 4:779.
12. *The Oxford English Dictionary*, ed. J. Murray et al. (Oxford: Oxford Univ. Press, 1933), 6:818.

Another such definition says that "myth is a story of the gods in which results of natural causes are accounted for supernaturally."[13] Obviously such a definition makes the assumption that all events have nothing but natural causes. Thus, it becomes impossible to speak truthfully while ascribing an event to divine causation. But this need not be the case. If there *is* a divine first cause, then to ascribe events to his activity is not necessarily to speak falsely. To say "God sent the rain" does not deny all of the meteorological causes and effects that go into rainfall, but it may be quite truthful in asserting that ultimately there was a distinct supernatural inception and guidance of the particular phenomena being described.

Yet another etymological definition takes us one step further afield. This one holds that "myth is a story involving a pre-scientific world-view."[14] There is a hint of cultural arrogance in this point of view in that it seems to say that it was impossible for a person with a prescientific worldview to speak truthfully about reality. Since they did not understand the mechanisms by which the world operates, their insights about the meaning and destiny of life were necessarily false. C. S. Lewis illustrates the fallacy of such an argument in his imaginary story about the little girl and "horrid red things."[15] The little girl tells a visitor in her home that he must never drink from a certain bottle marked with a skull and crossbones because it will kill him. When he inquires why it will have this dire effect, she assures him that it is because the liquid inside contains "horrid red things." Lewis then asks whether the visitor should not go ahead and drink the poison since the little girl's faulty understanding of the nature of poison obviously invalidated her report of its effects. Of course the answer is no.

The fact that the Hebrews may have shared with the Babylonians the idea that there were windows in the heavens through which, when they were opened, the rain poured, does not thereby mean that their report of Noah's involvement in the flood was necessarily fictional. The veracity of a narrative cannot be prejudged on the basis of whether supernatural causation or prescientific worldviews are involved.

---

13. M. Gaster, "Myth," *Interpreter's Dictionary of the Bible*, ed. G. Butterick (New York; Abingdon, 1962), 3:481.
14. R. Bultmann, "New Testament and Mythology," in *Kerygma and Myth I*, ed. H. Bartsch (London: SPCK, 1953), 1.
15. C. S. Lewis, *Miracles* (London: Collins, 1947), 75–76.

A final example of these kinds of definitions describes myth as fanciful as opposed to philosophical or speculative thought.[16] Rather than functioning according to Greek logic, it depends on free analogy. Thus for the Egyptians, the sun crossed the sky in a boat. Why? Because humans crossed the Nile in a boat. But, by the same token, the sun is a falcon. Why? Because the falcon soars across the sky. Now comes the rub. The Greek thinker says, "So the falcon crosses the sky in a boat." The mythmaker is stunned. "Why would you say such a silly thing? Of course the falcon does not cross the sky in a boat." The law of noncontradiction, which says that two things that equal the same thing must equal each other, is not applied. The assumption here is that the fanciful description is false while one that would describe the sun strictly in terms of naturalistic logic is "true."

Two comments need to be made about the etymological definitions of myth. First, it will not do to dismiss such meanings lightly as the territory of the unenlightened, as G. B. Caird seems to do.[17] Since this has been, and remains, the generally held definition, the burden of proof continues to rest on those who say it is incorrect. Furthermore, it is incumbent on them to explain why not only the Greeks, but the New Testament writers used the term in this way.[18]

But a second point needs to be made regarding the etymological definitions of myth, and that is that they are frequently too broad. To say that a myth is something false is one thing, but if one then limits "truth" to sensuous fact, or to natural causation, or to a mechanistic worldview, then we may well class as myth — false — two things that may have in common only the idea of supernatural causation and nothing else.

---

16. This is a summarization of the point made in H. Frankfort's *Before Philosophy* (London: Penguin, 1949). For a much more involved definition along these lines, see p. 16.

17. G. B. Caird, *The Language and Imagery of the Bible* (Philadelphia: Westminster, 1980), 219–20.

18. All of the occurrences of "myth" in the New Testament are in contexts where the writers are at pains to insist that the teachings of the gospel are true accounts and not false "myths" (1 Tim. 1:4; 4:7; 2 Tim. 4:4; Tit. 1:14; 2 Peter 1:16). For further discussion see F. F. Bruce, "Myth," *New International Dictionary of New Testament Theology*, ed. C. Brown (Grand Rapids, Zondervan, 1976), 2:643–47; P. E. Hughes, "Myth," *Evangelical Dictionary of Theology*, ed. W. Elwell (Grand Rapids: Baker, 1984), 747–49; J. Oswalt, "Myth," *Evangelical Dictionary of Biblical Theology*, ed. W. Elwell (Grand Rapids: Baker, 1996), 547–48.

Sociological-Theological Definitions

This then leads us to a second group of historical-philosophical definitions. We may call them the sociological-theological definitions. Here the ruling idea is diametrically opposite to that of those just discussed. In these definitions myth is not something false, but something profoundly true! This idea stems from the sociological approach that does not ask whether an idea *is* true, but only whether the proponents of that idea *consider* it to be true. So the sociologist notes that the mythmakers tell their stories to convey what is to them some truth about the world. Assumed here of course is the relativity of truth. If a people thinks something is true, then it *is* true, at least for them.

An example of such a definition is "that literary form which tells about other-worldly things in this-worldly concepts."[19] This means that the validity of the "this-worldly concepts," the vehicle being used, is of no significance. Whether those terms bear any relation to this-worldly reality is not a matter of discussion. Thus, such a definition equates the Bible's use of historical narrative with Babylon's use of nature cycles. Both are merely vehicles that are used to convey each culture's perception of reality. Both views are "myths," and each perception has as much right to be accepted and believed as the other.

Another such definition is "the central theory of any religion which its adherents regard as true." Henri Frankfort is using such a concept when he says that the Israelites have substituted the myth of the will of god for the myth of natural recurrence.[20] By his use of "myth" he is saying that the Israelites are expressing their view of reality in the language of personal relationships rather than in abstract logic. They are conveying what to them is "truth." For them the idea that God has purposes for human life and that the highest good for an individual or a culture is to come into line with those purposes is the unifying principle of life. It is their "myth."

These kinds of definitions are popular today, especially in America, where the relativity of truth has come to reign supreme. Allan Bloom delineated this situation powerfully in his book *The Closing of the American*

---

19. E. Dinckler, "Myth in the NT," *Interpreter's Dictionary of the Bible*, ed. G. Butterick (New York: Abingdon, 1962), 3:487.
20. Frankfort, *Before Philosophy*, 244.

Mind.[21] He pointed out that we have come to the place where it is highly repugnant to us to have it said that if certain things are true then others are false. Thus, to be able to call any religious tenet a myth is highly satisfying. It means that I do not have to investigate whether that tenet's assertions have any claim on my life or not. The decision is wholly mine. If I choose to grant it the status of truth for me, well and good; but if I choose not to accord it such status, equally well and good. On the face of it, this seems like the best of all possible worlds. I am truly the master of my fate. My truth is *the* truth.

But like most utopian dreams, the apple has a worm in it. For if all things are equally true, then all things are equally false and the meaning of life disintegrates in our hands. Of course, given the original association of the word "myth" with falseness, these sociological definitions also leave the user free to suggest that, yes, the believers think these ideas are true, but you and I know they are false. Thus the word permits us to make value judgments without appearing to do so. A very useful device.

Thus, we are faced again with a kind of definition that is impossibly broad. Suppose some religious structures do accord with reality while others do not. Shall we call both myth because the adherents of both consider them true? What about concord with fact? In ordinary life there is one sure way to evaluate any idea or conviction — does it agree with the facts? I may believe with all my heart that I am Napoleon, but if the facts do not support me, then I am not Napoleon. But especially in the theological world, "fact" is a *persona non grata*. The world of values and the world of facts are held to be mutually exclusive, a view that extends at least as far back as Immanuel Kant. Fact has to do with the senses, with things that can be weighed and measured, proven. Who can weigh love? Who can measure integrity? Who can prove faith?

But surely this is a false distinction. If I have in fact been unfaithful to my wife, she has every right to question my protestations of love; if I have in fact turned in someone else's term paper with my name on it, my claims of personal integrity are worth little; if in fact I leave God no place to show

---

21. A. Bloom, *The Closing of the American Mind* (New York: Simon and Schuster, 1987), esp. 194 – 216.

His care in my life, of what value is my assertion that I trust Him? So a definition of myth that ignores the need for verification must ultimately misunderstand what both religion and truth are about, let alone myth.

Literary Definitions

A third kind of historical-philosophical definition is what I am calling the literary definition. Once again, these kinds of definitions generally claim to make no value judgments about their material. Instead they describe a certain way of writing or speaking. Thus, myth is a narrative in which there is a deeply serious use of symbolism to convey profound realities.[22] For example, it might be said that Herman Melville's *Moby Dick* has "mythic" overtones. By this it is meant that the book is not merely about Captain Ahab's obsessive quest for a particular whale. Rather, Ahab and the whale are symbols whereby the writer can explore some of the realities of human life. To some extent all enduring narratives do this. But some writings develop their themes and symbols in such a way that those themes and symbols come to have a universal application as well as appeal. At their most powerful, such writings come to speak for the most deeply felt perceptions of a culture and become a central part of that culture, not only as an expression of it, but ultimately, as a shaper of it.

It is in this sense that it might be said such figures as George Washington and Abraham Lincoln have become "mythic" figures in America. They have become representative figures who represent what we like to think of as true about American culture in its formative epochs. Another example might be the myth of the endless frontier, a figure whose usefulness is now lost and whose loss we are still grappling with.

Obviously, the literary definitions of myth can be helpful, particularly as they enable us to differentiate between types of literature. Thus, it is clear that not all uses of symbol are mythic in nature. Even some intensely symbolic kinds of literature like allegory are not necessarily mythic. But is it helpful to classify as myth all literatures that use symbols in a serious way to convey profound realities? This is an especially pertinent question in light of the inescapable historic association of the word with factual falsehood.

---

22. Rogerson seems to include this kind of definition under his heading, "Myth as an Aspect of Creative Imagination," "Slippery Words," 11.

To say that *Moby Dick* has mythic overtones will create few problems, especially for those who understand the definition being used, because everyone knows that the symbols used were fictional. But what of Abraham Lincoln? Does it matter whether the accounts of Lincoln are fictional or not? Is his present significance merely to be a vehicle to express what we believe is so about us, or would like to believe is so about us?

The question is, of course, do we create our symbols or do our symbols create us? Put another way, do we create our own reality, or is reality of such a nature as to shape us, like it or not? If by speaking of the myth of Abraham Lincoln, I suggest that it is now a matter of indifference whether Lincoln lived or not, or that the stories now told of him need not have any basis in fact, then indeed this kind of an understanding of myth does contain a value judgment, one that is the more dangerous because it is so subtle. And, indeed, all too many uses of this definition do assume that mythic symbols have a tenuous relation to historical reality. All this means that once again such a definition is often too broad. It may take under its umbrella literatures whose only common ground is a certain use of symbolism while in every other respect, especially in their view of reality, they differ widely.

The thing that all three of the types of historical-philosophical definitions have in common is not only the critical evaluation of the material being described, as was mentioned at the outset. They also have in common too great a breadth. In each case, there is the possibility of including items in the category that have only one feature in common. To say that myths are "stories of the gods" will not do. Neither will it do to say that myths are "attempts to convey supernatural truth in natural language." Is this the most we can say? After a helpful review of the issue Oden can only say that there is agreement that a myth is "(1) a story, and (2) traditional — that is, transmitted, usually orally, within a communal setting; further these traditional stories must (3) deal with a character or characters who are more than merely human ... [and] that myths (4) treat events in remote antiquity."[23] Thus the definition Oden prefers is: "the traditional tales of the deeds of *daimones*: gods, spirits, and all sorts of supernatural or superhuman beings."[24] But

---

23. Oden, "Myth and Mythology (OT)," 4:949.
24. Ibid., 949. The quotation is from J. Fontenrose, *The Ritual Theory of Myth* (University of California Folklore Studies 18; Berkeley: Univ. of California Press, 1966), 54 – 55.

such a definition seems especially open to the criticism of excessive breadth. Nor is it clear how this definition is an improvement over "stories of the gods," which Oden specifically rejects. We must find a narrower kind of definition that will allow us to include in the category all those items that manifestly have much in common while excluding those items that clearly have only one or two features in common.

Phenomenological Definitions

This narrower definition is what Childs means by what he calls "a phenomenological definition." Phenomenological definitions grow out of an attempt to describe the common characteristics of that world literature that, for one reason or another, has been called myth. The ruling word here is "characteristics" rather than function or quality. The weakness of the historical-philosophical definitions is at this point: they describe how myth operates in society, or they make judgments about its relation to truth or falsehood. What they do not do is attempt to describe the phenomenon itself. Such an approach is, at least initially, more descriptive and less analytical. It studies the literatures themselves, looking for common literary features, common types of thought, or common approaches to reality that characterize them.

One of the common features of myths is the ascription of personality to nature. Weiser says, "[Myth] usually arises in the soil of natural religion in which those processes of nature which are impressive by their regular recurrence or their peculiarity are explained by means of personifying them and representing them as the fortunes of the gods."[25] Around the world cultures have faced the terror of nature. Although we in the modern West have insulated ourselves from this to some extent, it only takes some great natural disaster to remind us too of our helplessness. Like it or not, humanity is at the mercy of nature. How shall we deal with that? How shall we gain some measure of control over nature?

In most parts of the world the answer has been the same. When nature is looked at carefully, it exhibits some remarkably human characteristics. Much of the time it is orderly and quite predictable. The seasons come and

---

25. Weiser, *Introduction*, 58.

go; the sun rises and sets; the tides rise and fall all with predictable regularity. However, that is not always so. At times, just as humans sometimes do, nature seems to go berserk, and as a result human security, which is always fragile, is destroyed.

If this observation of the human-like character of nature is correct and if all things are ultimately one, as the human heart dearly wishes to believe, then the way to deal with nature is as we would deal with humanity. Thus, all over the world we find societies where the central cultural symbols are stories in which the forces of nature are given human personas[26] and in which the actions of nature are made both explicable and controllable.

Alongside these stories, and frequently interwoven with them, are other stories where the more abstract forces that also impinge on human existence are treated in the same way. Such forces are love and power and war, to name a few. Once again these powers are given human personas, thus making their vagaries susceptible to explanation according to normal human behavior, but also making them susceptible to manipulation and control through the retelling of the stories.

Another definition of the phenomenological sort describes myth as the expression of "an attempt to relate the actual to the ideal, the punctual to the continual."[27] As mentioned above, human security is tenuous at best. All of us can conceive of that ideal world where all things go according to plan, where social collapse never occurs, where all our needs are instantly met. In fact, reality is far different. Again, we in America have been able to insulate ourselves from many of the material insecurities that plague the rest of the world. Yet we have not been able to eliminate insecurity. From some points of view, we are more insecure than our forefathers.

So we can understand the concerns of the ancients. They could conceive of that ideal world that, although not a static one — it was teeming with activity — was yet continually ordered and unchanging. It was, of course, the world of the gods, a world that the visible one of humans

---

26. Note that "persona" originally referred to the masks worn by players in the Greek and Latin dramas.

27. Gaster, "Myth," 3:481.

and nature dimly reflected. The problem lay in how to make this earthly reflection cohere more perfectly with the primeval reality. How can we keep chaos, whether natural or political or social, at bay? It seems always to be at the door. How can we ensure the potency of our king? A king who can no longer engender children is also a king who no longer has the energy to govern, and the society that has a king like that is unlikely to survive for long in this hostile world.

How can we ensure fertility, our own as well as that of our animals and fields? For that which is sterile is dead in present potential and soon, in actual fact. If my seeds do not germinate or my sheep do not get pregnant, then I and my family will starve before another harvest comes. If my wife does not bear many sons and daughters, then it is unlikely that any will live to adulthood, and it will be as if my wife and I had never lived. Fertility is the only insurance against that greatest of all threats to human security — death.

Now in the ideal world, chaos is continually being defeated; the king is continually regaining his potency; and fertility is continually destroying sterility, as indeed the forces of life are continually conquering death. The problem is how to relate this actual world to that ideal world. The answer is the myth. In the very act of retelling the stories of these events in the divine world a connection is made. If, in addition, the stories are acted out, the relationship is that much more secure. That the retelling or the reenactment can have this effect depends on that analogical reasoning mentioned above. Since the retelling is like the supposed reality, therefore it *becomes* that reality on this earthly plane. Thus a common feature of myths is that they relate timeless stories in an effort to apply the outcomes of those stories to events of time.

This brings us to yet a third phenomenological definition. According to this one, myth's nature is to ignore fetters of time and space, gazing into the widest vistas and launching out into the exalted and immense.[28] This definition results from the observation that a common feature of myths is a specific disinterest in what we know as history. Reflection on the previous point makes it clear why this is so. Reality is believed to reside in the ideal

---

28. A. Weiser, *The Old Testament* (New York: Association, 1961), 58.

world, not this one. Thus individual persons and events are only significant insofar as they partake of the ideal. In and of themselves, especially as they may be unique, they have no significance at all. Myth is interested in principles, forces, cycles, the immense, and the numinous. Particular and mundane events in time and space are specifically not of interest to the mythmaker. They do not tell us of the great recurring cycles, and furthermore, the telling of them might disturb those cycles.

Yes, the stories of human heroes may be told, but these heroes are not presented as particular individuals. Rather they are presented as symbols. These heroes have been lifted out of common time and space so that they can become representative of the race or of the aspirations and limitations of the race. They are only real insofar as they are not particular. In the mythic world, the individual and particular things about an event are precisely those things that separate it from reality. What is real about the person or the thing is that in it which partakes of the limitless and the unchanging.

The Centrality of Continuity

How shall we sum up these descriptive definitions of myth? At heart, they all recognize one central feature that explains the several common features. Around the world, those literatures that express the deepest perceptions of a people or a culture tend to share the worldview of "continuity" or "correspondence."[29] Continuity is a philosophical principle that asserts that all things are continuous with each other. Thus I am one with the tree, not merely symbolically or spiritually, but actually. The tree is me; I am the tree. The same is true of every other entity in the universe, including deity. This means that the divine is materially as well as spiritually identical with the psycho-socio-physical universe that we know. Of course this idea exists in many variations, but the core idea remains the same, and it is found in

---

29. "Correspondence" is the term used by Y. Kaufmann in the extremely helpful discussion in his book *The Religion of Israel*, trans. M. Greenberg (Chicago: Univ. of Chicago Press, 1960), esp. 1 – 150. It is also used by J. Barr in "The Meaning of 'Mythology' in Relation to the Old Testament," *Vetus Testamentum* 9 (1959): 1 – 10. For a similar, recent expression of these ideas, see H. Brichto, *The Names of God* (New York: Oxford Univ. Press, 1996), 57 – 70.

all the great religious literatures of the world, except the Israelite one and its three derivatives, Judaism, Christianity, and Islam.

This principle of continuity explains all the commonalities of myth that we have discussed above. It requires no suspension of the intellect to ascribe human personality to natural forces if indeed nature and humanity are continuous with each other. In fact, for those who accept continuity, the opposite is true. To deny personality to nature would be intellectually contradictory and a heresy of the gravest degree.

By the same token, continuity undergirds the idea that the retelling or the reenactment of a story secures the effects of the story for the present. The story *is* the event, and through the story the event is now. Thus, when the mythical story of creation is reenacted on the first day of the new annual cycle, the triumph of order over disorder that is continually occurring in the invisible world of the gods is actualized for this new year. Apart from that principle the reenactment of the story would serve no purpose at all.

Finally, continuity explains myth's disinterest in the particular. If my maleness is stressed, this makes me discontinuous with the female part of existence. If my blue eyes are stressed, this makes me discontinuous with the brown-eyed part of existence, and so forth. But to the extent that I am discontinuous with existence I do not exist. Therefore it is what I share in common with all that is truly significant about me. And the highest end of existence is that all its particular expressions might one day lose their particularities and be absorbed back into the All.

Kaufmann takes this one step farther when he points out that the basis of this continuity or correspondence is what he calls "the meta-divine," the shapeless, nameless power that inhabits the cosmos and is the basis of all things. It is this power that conditions the actions of the gods and it is this power that the worshiper attempts to manipulate to control the gods (as they attempt to manipulate it to control one another). So he says, "This is the great symbol of paganism's fundamental idea: the existence of a realm of power to which the gods themselves are subject."[30]

What, then, is myth? How shall we define it? First of all, it is not a question of whether it is true or false, or whether those who tell it think it is true

---

30. Kaufmann, *The Religion of Israel*, 22.

or false. None of these value judgments describe the common characteristics of the thing itself. Furthermore, while functional definitions help by showing how the thing is used, such definitions must be explicit or they run the risk of confusing different things. A hammer and a hatchet may both be used to pound a nail, but that does not mean they are the same thing.

These kinds of confusions are rampant today when the Bible is compared to ancient myth. It is all too easy to say that the Bible is myth because its adherents consider it true, or because it provides the central set of images and symbols for the Jewish and Christian religions, or because it ascribes to the divine the results of natural causation. Certainly the Bible does the first two, and if it is correctly understood, it does the latter as well. But that does not mean it is myth. An elephant is not a table because it has four legs. The reason these equations between the two types of literature can be made is that they rest on definitions that fail to deal seriously with the characteristic thought patterns of the two.

In fact, as the phenomenological definitions intimate, myth is best characterized by its common understanding of, and approach to, the world. Above everything else this approach involves continuity. Myth depends for its whole rationale on the idea that all things in the cosmos are continuous with each other. Furthermore, myth exists to actualize that continuity. Thus mythical descriptions of the gods invariably depict them as human in every respect, only more so. They are strong; they are weak; they are good; they are bad; they are trustworthy; they are fickle. All that humanity is, the gods are. And how could it be otherwise in a cosmos of continuity?

What then is myth? This is Childs' phenomenological definition:

> Myth is a form by which the existing structure of reality is understood and maintained. It concerns itself with showing how an action of a deity, conceived of as occurring in the primeval age, determines a phase of contemporary world order. Existing world order is maintained through the actualization of the myth in the cult.[31]

Thus, myth is a form of expression, whether literary or oral, whereby the continuities among the human, natural, and divine realms are expressed

---

31. Childs, *Myth and Reality*, 27 – 28.

and actualized. By reinforcing these continuities, it seeks to ensure the orderly functioning of both nature and human society. If this definition is accepted, then it must be abundantly clear that whatever the Bible is, it is not myth. It is not a question of the Bible being true and myth being false, or vice versa. Nor is it a question of the Bible's using historical symbols while the myths use nature symbols.

The fact is that the Bible has a completely different understanding of existence and of the relations among the realms. As a result, it functions entirely differently. Its telling does not actualize continuous divine reality out of the real invisible world into this visible reflection of that reality. Rather, it is a rehearsal of the nonrepeatable acts of God in identifiable time and space in concert with human beings. Its purpose is to provoke human choices and behavior through the medium of memory. Nothing could be farther from the purpose of myth. Whatever the Bible is, whether true or false, symbol or literal, it is not myth. In the next chapter we will explore the concept of continuity further and show how the biblical concept of reality differs radically.

CHAPTER 3

CONTINUITY: THE BASIS OF MYTHICAL THINKING

I concluded the preceding chapter with the statement that whatever the Bible is, it is not myth. That is to say, I have concluded that the similarities between the Bible and the rest of the literatures of the ancient Near East are superficial, while the differences are essential. I led up to that statement through an analysis of various definitions for myth, concluding with those I have called phenomenological, because they seek to define the phenomenon through a study of its distinctive characteristics rather than through evaluation.

In this chapter, I want to continue that process of analyzing the thought world of myth, for it is not ultimately the fabulous details found in many myths that mark a piece of literature as myth. When all is said and done, it is a particular way of looking at reality. First, we will look at the general characteristics of this way of thinking about reality, and then we will look at the common features that this kind of thinking gives rise to in the literature.

At the outset it must be emphasized that when we talk about the common worldview of myth, we are not talking about a quaint, outgrown idea without relevance to the present. Myth is not the thought of primitives who cannot think of reality in abstract terms. It is simply a way of thinking about reality different from the one that has shaped Western thought. Nor is this kind of thinking impossible for "enlightened" thinkers. In fact, as I will show in a later chapter, this understanding of reality is increasingly common in the modern, technological world. We dress it differently, but beneath the new clothes, it is the same body as that which has existed for thousands of years. This means that the conflict between it and the biblical worldview is as inescapable and as urgent today as it has ever been.

CONTINUITY AS THE RULING CONCEPT IN MYTH

As the previous chapter maintained, the ruling idea in the worldview that gives myth its distinctive character is continuity. This is the idea that all things that exist are part of each other. Thus, there are no fundamental distinctions between the three realms: humanity, nature, and the divine. The cosmos looks like this:

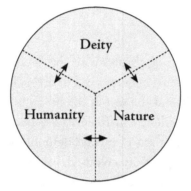

Everything that exists is within the circle, and everything in the circle is coexistent with everything else in it. This is why the lines between the three segments are dotted. There is a community of essence among the various elements, and each segment partakes of the other two. So gods are humans and natural forces; nature is divine and divinity has human-like characteristics; humanity is divine and is one with nature. There is no distinction in nature among the three, only one in roles.[1]

This idea has a number of far-reaching implications. For instance, it means that things that look the same or sound the same *are* the same. So, since the idol is like Baal, it *is* Baal. What is done to the idol is done to Baal. But Baal is also like the storm: he is potent; he is life-giving; he is impetuous; he is destructive. Therefore, he *is* the storm. Thus, what is done to Baal is done to the storm, and what is done to the storm is done to Baal. In this way, assuming that no barriers have been erected between the realms by destructive forces, it is possible to exert a measure of control over the divine

---

1. This diagram was originally shared with me by my professor Dr. G. Herbert Livingston. His book *The Pentateuch in Its Cultural Environment* (Grand Rapids: Baker, 1974), 85 – 135, has a helpful discussion of this subject.

and nature. But perhaps equally important, this understanding also means that humans can participate in nature and in the divine.

The idea of continuity also means that there is no distinction between symbol and reality; the symbol *is* the reality. To be sure, the visible world is only a reflection of the invisible, divine world, but as its reflection it is identical with it. A popular term for this idea is pantheism: the divine is everything and everything is the divine. Hinduism is perhaps the most developed expression of this thought. Perhaps a slightly more accurate term for this way of thinking about reality, especially as it appears in the ancient Near East and most other cultures, is "pan-en-theism": everything is within the divine. The fundamental point, however, is that all things that exist are physically and spiritually part of one another. This is the single most important aspect of the way of thinking that characterizes myth.

ORIGINS AND IMPLICATIONS OF CONTINUITY

Where does such an idea come from? We receive a clue in the observation that myths are tied to the "status quo."[2] They have two chief concerns: explaining why things are as they are now, and maintaining things as they are now. These concerns spring directly out of the human terror of chaos. We are afraid of chaos because it always destroys our security, and security is perhaps the greatest of all human longings. If we are to gain the security we so desperately want, the first order of the day is some sense of intellectual order. If we can explain why things are as they are, then we have that sense of intellectual order, and we also have the feeling that we know how to relate to the thing explained.

Interestingly enough, one possibility that the mythmakers consistently neglect is the analysis of human choices and behaviors in the past to see how those might have shaped the present. Why do they do this? It is a logical outcome of the conviction of continuity. If I am really one with all humans, then I really have no choices of my own. And oftentimes life seems to bear that out. We do things for reasons that we do not understand, and we experience results that often seem to have little relationship to what we

---

2. See B. S. Childs, *Myth and Reality in the Old Testament* (London: SCM, 1960), 19–21.

did or chose to do. So we feel that our actions have little bearing on the real outcome of things.

As a result, given that human choices and actions have little bearing on what really happens in our lives, how are we to achieve these goals of security, survival, comfort, and pleasure? Or, to put it another way, how can I explain the world in such a way as to maintain it to my greatest advantage? The approach found everywhere is to project present reality onto the ultimate. The only way to explain the particular characteristics of the visible world is to suppose that there is an invisible world of ultimate reality and that it takes the same shape as the visible one. The mythmaker thus reasons from the given to the divine. But this is only possible if there is a continuity, or correspondence, between the visible realms of humanity and nature and the divine realm. If there is a radical discontinuity between this realm and the one that explains it, then we are truly helpless — at the mercy of the gods — and this is something the human spirit cannot bear.

Thus, continuity serves both an intellectual and a practical function. If this world and the other world are continuous, then we can affect that other world by what we do here. We are not helpless; we can act out what we want the gods to do and it will be done, not because they must do it, but because in our very actions they *are* doing it. They and we are one. This oneness is always potentially so, but the performance of certain rituals, themselves expressive of continuity, reinforces the reality.

Reality Only Relates to the Present

This reasoning from the given to the divine, which can only be done on the basis of the assumption of continuity, has a number of implications for the thought patterns involved. First, such concepts as past and future have no real value to the mythmaker. "Now," the present, is all that exists, and thus reality only relates to the present. To be sure, the origins of all things are to be found in the acts of the gods in primal time, but that is not yesterday or the day before. Those events are outside of time altogether. Furthermore, the idea of a future when things will not be as they are now plays no part in the myths. We do not find stories of utopian realms where the sun always shines and there is no war and everyone eats simply by plucking grapes from a vine. Rather, the myths speak of those primeval events that undergird what now is. In them are found conflict and resolution, love and hate, hope and despair, life and death.

This is the stuff of reality, and there is no basis for imagining some other reality. "Now" is all there is, all we have by which to explain reality. Time has always rolled and it always will, but it is going nowhere. The task is to find ways of ensuring that it does not stop rolling or that it does not roll in some completely unforeseen way.[3]

Actualization of Timeless Reality

This maintenance is accomplished, as mentioned above, through actualization of the timeless reality. Suppose the rains do not come when they should in the normal cycle of things. How can we explain this, and even more important, what can we do about it? Reasoning from the given to the divine we can understand that heaven and earth are male and female. Plant and animal life are the result of divine copulation, for all things in this world that we know have their origins in sexual behavior. Therefore, the thing to do is to get the god and goddess to have sexual relations. If they do, then the rain will fall into the womb of the earth and fertilize it.

How do we do that? By asking them to do so, or trusting them to do so? Far from it! We do it for them through ritual enactment. As the worshiper and the priestess have sex together under the appropriate ritual circumstances, the god and goddess do so as well and the rhythms of nature are maintained. This is why prostitution has always been the domain of the temples.[4] Sexual activity is much too important to the maintenance of existence to leave to the merely mundane.

---

3. Mircea Eliade, in his *Myth and Reality* (New York: Harper & Row, 1963), 50 – 53, proposed that mythmakers seek to return to a primeval realm of bliss. But apart from the biblical account of Eden, his evidence seems very indeterminate. The myth of Enki and Ninhursag (*ANET*, 37 – 41) mentions the paradisiacal land of Dilmun, but it is not at all clear what the function of that land is in the overall narrative. In the biblical account, there is no clear evidence that there is a desire for a return to Eden. The Old Testament evinces no such thing, and the New Testament vision of eternal life is of something much better than Eden.

4. There is now argument that we do not know for certain how temple prostitution functioned. See most recently S. Budin, *The Myth of Sacred Prostitution in Antiquity* (Cambridge: Cambridge Univ. Press, 2008). This does not alter the fact that prostitution was managed out of the temples through women and men dedicated to the temple and its gods.

But we should not think that this way of ensuring fertility is the only means of doing so. There are other correspondences which may be observed, and they may function just as well to achieve the desired results. So we may think of the death and rebirth of plant life in terms of the death and rebirth of the gods. Indeed, this theme of death and rebirth may be expressed in several different, even mutually contradictory, ways in the same culture. The idea of logical consistency based on the concept of the unity of reality is simply not a part of this way of thinking. The point is that if the correspondences can be found and if they can be recounted in such a way as to make them effective for achieving the desired results, that is all that is necessary.

Blurring of Source and Manifestation

This blurring of the one and the many and of the source and the manifestation is common to all myths. The Shatapatha Brahamana contains a typical expression of this when it says, "He is one as he is there, but many as he is in his children here."[5] The Egyptians express a similar concept when they say that Amon-Re is the "one" who is hidden from all the gods and yet assert that he has a thousand faces. What both of these are saying is that ultimate reality can be one and not-one at the same time. If the realms of humanity and nature are congruent with the divine realm, then it is impossible to think of there being any exclusive unity in reality. The realms of humanity and nature are irreducibly multiplex, at least to all appearances, so the divine realm must be equally multiplex.

While it is theoretically possible to conceive of a oneness within the multiplicity, such a oneness has little bearing on this world that we are seeking to maintain in order. As a result, while oneness remains an abstract possibility, it is the multiplicity that becomes dominant in practice. This fact is seen in the Indian and Egyptian societies whose theological statements were just cited. The religions of these two societies are among the most polytheistic in the world. The multiplicity of the manifestations is much more significant for manipulating reality than is the theoretical oneness of the source.

---

5. Cited in J. Campbell, *The Mythic Image* (Princeton: Princeton Univ. Press, 1975), 6.

The lack of distinction that we are discussing here can be stated in more abstract terms as a denial of the subject-object distinction. The subject is me and the object is something apart from me that I can contemplate. All science is based on this distinction. I am not the experiment, and if the experiment does not come out according to my expectations, I do not falsify the report in order to escape being diminished. That is, I do not do so if I am a good scientist. Why not? Because science believes that there is a reality that exists apart from me. That reality is so whether I like it or not, and it is ultimately in my best interests to discover what it is so I can relate rightly to it.

But for the mythmaker, such a distinction makes no sense. If there is anything that is discontinuous with me, it is meaningless. If it is truly separate from me, it does not exist for me; I cannot participate in its life and it cannot participate in mine. Things only have meaning for me as they relate to me. It is pointless to make a distinction between me the subject and something that is not-me. What else is there but me the subject? Of what importance is anything except as it relates to me?

When this understanding is projected on the divine, the result is obvious. Deity must be part of me as I must be part of it. To say that I am not divine, or that the divine is not me, or to say that the deity is not the world, or that the world is not the deity, is to make life uncontrollable and meaningless. As the source the divine is the subject, but as the manifestation it is the object. Because of continuity, it must be both at once. To distinguish between the source and the manifestation is to make the source unreachable through the manifestation, a circumstance that is highly undesirable. We will develop this thought more fully in a later chapter.

This blurring of source and manifestation is what underlies the story of the golden calf. Since Moses was worshiping the invisible One, the source, on the mountain, why should not the people worship one of his visible manifestations as a part of the Many in the valley? So God could be the invisible Creator and the visible created (the bull) at one and the same time. The text shows us that this is how they were thinking when it tells us that Aaron said of the image, "Behold your God [Heb. ʾelohim] who brought you forth from Egypt" (Ex. 34:4; lit. trans.).

Aaron and the people did not consider themselves to be doing anything heretical. After all, this is religion as they had observed it in Egypt for years.

As the source, God is One, and other than creation. But as a manifestation he is many and a part of creation. The mythmaker sees no contradiction. But Moses understood that the God who was revealing himself to the Israelites was somehow distinctly other than creation. Thus, no blurring of God and creation could be allowed to exist. To permit it to exist would be to deny the nature of reality as Yahweh was revealing it to his people.

Importance of Nature Symbolism

The concept of continuity with its consequent reasoning from the given to the divine also means that myth always uses nature symbolism as the key expression of the divine. G. S. Kirk is certainly right when he says that many of the explanations we give of the relations between nature and the myths are both too easy and too hard.[6] He means by this that the ways in which the mythmakers felt the relationships were undoubtedly much more subliminal than we can conceive of. Thus our involved rational explanations of the ritual would be much too complicated for them, but at the same time our explanations would miss the mysterious and the numinous elements involved.

But granted the rightness of Kirk's observations, it is still correct to note that the gods were all personified forces, mostly natural ones, although a few were social forces. This is especially true of the great gods. Heaven, earth, sun, moon, stars, rain, wind, fire, storm, vegetation, death, fertility, passion — all of these are represented at the top of any pantheon around the world. Why? Because these are the forces that need to be explained and ordered if life in the here and now is to be maintained. And since these forces are the keys to life in this realm, it is obvious that they must hold similar places in the divine realm.

Significance of Magic

If we understand the human, the natural, and the divine worlds as all being a part of one another, then magic, especially sympathetic, or imitative, magic comes to have great significance. Magic may be defined as "the use of means (such as charms or spells) believed to have supernatural power

---

6. G. S. Kirk, *Myth: Its Meaning and Functions in Ancient and Other Cultures* (Cambridge: Cambridge Univ. Press, 1970), 89 – 90.

over natural forces."[7] To accomplish something in the natural or divine realms is a matter of doing a similar thing in this human realm. Getting what you want is a matter of learning the right techniques. If you perform the techniques in the right way, then the desired results must follow.

However, the linkages between the realms (the arrows in the diagram above) are capable of being disturbed, and there are chaotic forces in the universe that would like to see just that happen. This is where the unclean and the demonic enter in. Unless great care is taken to rid an area, or a utensil, or even a ritual, of the unclean, the magic will not work. Any study of magic rites from any part of the world will show that simplistic, rational explanations cannot account for all that is done, nor can one-to-one equations be made between the behaviors and the results. Centuries of tradition lie behind each practice. Furthermore, as was said just above, these rituals rest on connections that are more felt and intuited than they are reasoned. But be that as it may, magic is central to myth.

Obsession with Fertility and Potency

Finally, myths, being the result of reasoning from the given to the divine, are obsessed with fertility and potency. This is hardly surprising when we consider the centrality of sexuality and sexual behavior to human life. Beyond that, sex is the one of all the physical desires that seems to be most related to the psyche and is thus most absorbing. It follows, then, that sex and sexuality, along with fertility and potency, should be integral to ultimate reality. This perception expresses itself in a number of different ways. One of these is the prominence of the worship of the bull and other sexually potent animals. Another is the cult of the mother goddess as represented by figurines and drawings in which the physical sexual features of the goddess are exaggerated, sometimes grossly. Ritual prostitution has already been mentioned.[8]

---

7. "Magic," *Merriam-Webster's Collegiate Dictionary*, 10th ed. (Springfield, MA: Merriam-Webster, 2000), 697.

8. The evidence from the Bible is not to be gainsaid. There were women "who were available." Such a woman was a *zonah*. But there were the sacred prostitutes, and it was as one of these, a *qadešah*, that Tamar dressed herself to have sex with her father-in-law, Judah, on his way to the shearing floor (Gen. 38). She was not a "woman of the night."

Perhaps the most widespread expression of this obsession with sexuality and fertility in the ancient Near East was the cult of the dying and rising god. In the Sumerian religion as well as in those that followed it — the Babylonian, the Egyptian, the Canaanite, the Hittite, the Greek, and the Roman — one of the cycles of myths tells how the vegetation or fertility god was killed by the god of death, with the corresponding death of all the plant and animal life. Through the ministrations of the dead god's consort, who is variously his mother, his wife, his sister, or his mistress, and sometimes all of the above (distinctions serve no purpose in a world of continuity), the god is restored to life and nature is rejuvenated. Scholars are divided over whether this myth was reenacted each fall, but the reference in Ezekiel to the temple women weeping for Tammuz, the Babylonian vegetation god, suggests that in Jerusalem at least, this was an annual event.

Denial of Boundaries

Clearly, if continuity is the correct explanation of reality, and if continuity is to function as we wish, then boundaries between the realms, and even within them, are not permissible. If there is any kind of a boundary between humans and gods, or between the gods and nature, then the rituals will not work, and we humans are left with no way to affect our destinies. This denial of boundaries is especially seen in the sexual domain. The practice of ritual prostitution was far from the only expression of sexuality in connection with the cult. Incest, bestiality, and homosexual prostitution were also practiced. Juvenal, the Roman writer, who was hardly a prude, refers to the temples as cesspools, where every corruption was practiced.[9]

Why was this so? Was it an unfortunate aberration? Hardly. It is a theological statement. If continuity is to work, both as a philosophical and a practical principle, then there can be no boundaries anywhere in the cosmos. There can be no boundaries between parent and child (hence, incest); there can be no boundaries around marriage (hence, prostitution);[10] there

---

9. *Juvenal and Persius*, trans. G. G. Ramsey, rev. ed. (Loeb Classical Library; Cambridge, MA: Harvard Univ. Press, 1940), 109–11.

10. The Roman author Lucius reports that in the Phoenician city of Byblos, every woman had to prostitute herself to a stranger for one day during the festival of Adonis (Baal) or else

can be no boundaries between members of the same sex (hence, homosexual behavior); there can be no boundaries between humans and animals (hence, bestiality). All these practices were told and acted out in the myths.

They are not primitive behaviors, nor are they, as some maintain, the result of urban sophistication. They are theological statements, necessary expressions of the worldview of which they are a part. Once you allow boundaries anywhere in the cosmos, it becomes impossible for me to control things, to manipulate reality, through the use of magic. It is as though a hydraulic system had a shut-off valve between the master cylinder and the slave cylinder. Until that shut-off valve is taken out and there is a direct connection between the two cylinders, the system will not work.

COMMON FEATURES OF MYTHS

Polytheism

With these general characteristics of the worldview of myth in mind, we can understand more easily why certain specific features characterize myths. First, myth is invariably polytheistic. Of course there are many gods if we are explaining the divine in terms of this world. There are many different forces in this world and there must be a god for each one. This is not an accidental characteristic but an essential one. The world is an emanation of the divine and the world is multiplex. Therefore, there must be many gods.

Images

Second, the gods are always represented by images in the shapes of this world. The idol is an ideal representative of continuity. First of all it is a part of nature, whether made of wood or stone or some other natural material; second, it is commonly in the form of a human; and third, it is ritually invested with the names and trappings of a particular god. Thus the typical idol is at the same time divine, human, and nature. Furthermore, by doing things to the idol, one is simultaneously doing things to the god or goddess and to the natural force he or she inhabits.

---

be shorn of her hair; *On the Syrian Goddess*, trans. H. Strong, ed. J. Garstang (London: Constable, 1913), 15.

Eternity of Chaotic Matter

Third, myths assume that matter is the fundamental element that has always existed, the essential constituent of the universe. Thus, in every mythical account of beginnings in the ancient Near East, the first thing, the thing that has always been, is chaotic matter. Out of this matter come the first gods, who in turn form the chaos into the present order. Often this chaotic matter is vaguely female, but it is never personal, even to the degree that the gods are. All of this is fully understandable if we recognize that the myths are the result of reasoning from the present cosmos to ultimate reality. If our human experience is the given, then it is plain that the all-pervasive element in that experience is matter. Thus, matter has always existed and always will.[11] To be sure, spirit animates the matter, but matter is the base.

Personality Not Essential to Reality

But fourth, although matter is always animate, it is not necessarily personal. Again, the reasons are clear. While spirit may be assumed for both nature and humanity, personality is found only in humanity. That being so, it is unreasonable to expect that the divine realm should be distinctively personal. Personality also presents a problem for continuity: personalities tend to distinguish persons from one another rather than unite them. Thus, it is not surprising to discover that the deities in the mythical pantheons are not fully personal, but represent personalized forces. By that I mean we do not find full-orbed persons in the gods and goddesses, acting and reacting on a multidimensional level. Rather, the characters and their responses tend to be flat and stereotyped. Like the characters in a Greek drama, one senses that the human personas of the gods are only masks worn to make the forces that they represent more intelligible.

Low View of the Gods

Fifth, the myths take a uniformly low view of the gods. The gods are untrustworthy, seeking their own ends rather than caring for their wor-

---

11. Note that this is the fundamental assumption of "modern" science. We have not come very far from the Sumerians in Mesopotamia in 3000 BC, among whom this idea was first expressed in writing.

shipers' ends. They are constantly fighting among each other, often over the most petty matters. They are fearful, especially of death, but they can do nothing lasting about their fears, for each of them, like the stars in their orbits, are fixed to a certain fate. They are limited, both in knowledge and in power. They are subject to magic, both that of the worshipers and that which they may apply to each other. All of this may be summed up by saying that the gods are not absolute. If there is an absolute in the myths, and one is always dimly sensed, then it is that raw impersonal power (Kaufmann's "meta-divine") that is behind everything; that which magic seeks to tap into and utilize; that to which the gods themselves are subject and which they seek to use against each other.

Conflict Is the Source of Life

In the myths, conflict is the source of life. There is never-ending conflict between the forces of construction and the forces of chaos. The cosmos itself is the result of such a primal conflict between chaotic matter and the gods whom she has spawned. In the Mesopotamian version of the story, Chaos recognizes that the rapidly reproducing gods are not going to leave her alone and so she sets out to kill them. In self-defense they destroy her and use her body as raw material to make the present cosmos. The names and details change, but the same ideas recur in myth after myth around the world. In the ancient Near East, up to and including Rome, the theme may have been borrowed from culture to culture, going back to the earliest we know, the Sumerians.

But what of other parts of the world, where no such borrowing is possible? Here the only way to account for the similarities is to recognize that if one starts with this cosmos and reasons from it to the ultimate realities, then one will get basically the same results, whether the reasoner is an Australian aborigine or a Hindu Brahmin.

Low View of Humanity

The list of commonalities goes on: there is a uniformly low view of humanity in myth. Humans were created to serve the gods, and to a significant degree their creation was an afterthought. In the Babylonian creation myth they are created to feed the gods after the gods have been fixed in heaven and can no longer care for themselves. In one of the Egyptian versions humans are merely the tears of Atum that fell into the dust during his struggle with Chaos. It is not hard to understand where such an understanding comes from if we are reasoning from life as we see it. Humans seem insignificant when we look at the world of nature.

Furthermore, humans have no real control over their destinies, or so it appears. Choice seems to be an illusion. Given the fact that this visible realm is but a reflection of the real invisible realm, one must merely play the part that is given to a person with as much nobility as is possible. Since there is no choice, of course there is no responsibility. Your fate may be good or bad, but that has little to do with you. Even in Hinduism, the hope of one day getting off the wheel of existence and being absorbed back into nothingness is a small hope. If you are a low-caste person, there is no way you can better your lot in this life; you are locked in, doomed by something unknown and unremembered, and probably insignificant on anything but a magical level.

If humanity is insignificant, then individual humans are truly insignificant. In a worldview of continuity individual elements only have significance to the degree that they reflect the norm. But what makes us individual is precisely the degree to which we vary from the norm. Thus, our individual characteristics, our unique personalities, are of no importance. The individual drop of water is nothing; it is only the ocean that truly matters. So it is that which we have in common with everyone else that is truly important. This, of course, accords with the law of continuity. We exist in that we reflect the ideal humanity. Our differences from that ideal do not make us someone special; they make us nobody. Thus, the casual attitude toward individual human beings in much of the world is not the result of some calculated brutality; it is the result of a way of thinking about reality.

No Single Standard of Ethics

In myth, there is no single standard of ethics. Again, reasoning from the given to the divine would not allow such a thing. There are many gods and goddesses and each of these gods has varying likes and dislikes. Furthermore, the visible world did not come into existence as a result of any divine will or purpose. As a result, it becomes impossible to say that there is a single standard of right and wrong that is everywhere applicable. What one god wants, another god hates. So it clear that there cannot be any single standard of ethical behavior that has some universal divine warrant behind it.

Nevertheless, it is a given that no society can survive for long unless all its members subscribe to a single standard of ethics. Thus, we find in the Mesopotamian and Hittite societies several law codes that are now more or less well known.[12] These standards were frequently given force by having it said that they derived from a god. But obedience to these standards was not a religious obligation. Indeed, ethics and religion had no practical connection in the end. Ethics were a social and civil matter only.

Cyclical Concept of Existence

A final common feature of myths that I wish to mention is the cyclical concept of existence. Life as most persons know it in actual experience is a series of cycles that do not show any obvious progress. The most immediate one is the 24-hour day, and the next most immediate is the 365-day year. But there is another cycle that is less obvious, but is equally pervasive. It is one most of us do not like to think much about. This is the one that extends from nonexistence to dependence to independence to dependence to nonexistence. It is the cycle of life.

Thus, it is not surprising that world myth is uniform in imagining reality to be a continually turning wheel that comes from nowhere and goes nowhere. The past is only significant insofar as it shows us continuities that will repeat themselves. Thus, omens are of great importance. At some time in the past the shape of the entrails of a sacrificial animal coincided with some significant event. If that shape should present itself again, we may expect the same events to happen again. Thus the past will repeat itself and it is helpful to have information on hand to plan for that repetition. But the idea that the past might be transcended and that hitherto unknown events

---

12. They are the codes of Ur-Nammu (Sumerian, 2100 BC), Lipit-Ishtar (Sumerian, 1850), Eshnunna (Akkadian, 1800), and Hammurapi (Akkadian, 1700). In addition, there are the Hittite laws (1350) and the Middle Assyrian laws (1150). (See ANET for translations.) To date no comparable law codes have been found in Egypt. Some theorize that this is because of the theocratic nature of the Egyptian kingdoms, with the "god" being able to give ethical decrees by fiat.

could occur is not within the mythmaker's concept of reality. The shape of reality is determined by "now," and "now" is going nowhere.

In this chapter we have considered the phenomenon of myth. We have considered the common features that occur in the myths of the ancient Near East up to and including the Roman myths. But it is a fact that similar features can be found in myths from other places than the Near East. We have suggested that this is because all of them begin with the same starting point — the visible world — and operate on the same premise: this world takes the shape it does because it is a mirror image of the invisible world. Hinduism sees this world as a dream of Vishnu. Plato saw it as an almost endless series of reflections, with each one getting a little farther from reality. If one begins with this world and assumes the principle of continuity, as all of the world's myths do, it should not be surprising if the results of the process are remarkably similar. What I am saying is that there is a common principle of knowledge underlying mythmaking. That principle is that humans may discover ultimate reality by extrapolating from their own experience upon the assumption that their experience is identical with that reality. When they do that, they arrive, all over the world, at a remarkably similar understanding of reality.

CHAPTER 4

TRANSCENDENCE:
BASIS OF BIBLICAL THINKING

When we compare the characteristics described in the previous chapter with what we find in the Bible, it becomes clear that on every one of these points the biblical worldview differs — and not merely slightly, but diametrically. I am not arguing at this point that one worldview is more correct than the other. The time for that discussion is later. Here I am simply saying that any straightforward comparison must conclude that beneath any possible surface similarities are radically different ways of thinking about reality.[1]

The source for the data is the Old Testament as it stands now. The points being made are not dependent on any theory of the Bible's origins. Specifically they do not depend on any conviction concerning the factuality of any historical statements in the Bible. If we were to conclude that none of the biblical documents existed in any form before 400 BC and that the bulk of their historical statements are false, the data of the biblical worldview would still be the same. From start to finish the Old Testament is remarkably self-consistent regarding the things it maintains about the nature of reality. That recognition may have an impact on our conclusions concerning the Bible's origins and its veracity, but those conclusions in no way create the observations below. Those observations are simply facts, and they remain facts regardless of how we might explain them.

---

1. Recent attempts to deny that the concepts I will discuss in this chapter are genuinely different from those of myth are made in large part because to admit their difference then begins to point to a different origin for the biblical material, something unacceptable for many scholars. I want the reader to consider the data on its own and let subsequent questions remain subsequent.

COMMON CHARACTERISTICS OF
BIBLICAL THOUGHT

Monotheism

The single most obvious difference between the thought of the Old Testament and that of Israel's neighbors is monotheism. The Old Testament vehemently and continuously insists that Yahweh is one and that no other being is in the same category with him.[2] But sometimes today it is said that since Israel still believes in a divine being, there is not really all that much difference from the surrounding cultures. But this will not do. How many monotheistic religions are there in the world today? There are only three: Judaism, Christianity, and Islam. And where do these three get their monotheism? All from one source: the Old Testament.

This means that only once in the history of the world has a culture contrived to attain and maintain the idea of the absolute unity of deity.[3] On every side of it peoples far more brilliant than Israel were maintaining with vehemence the multiplicity of deity. Israel alone insisted on the oneness of God, even in the end to the death if necessary. Where did they come up with such an idea, and even more important, how did they maintain it in the face of all the evidence for multiplicity in the world around?

---

2. It may be objected that at a number of points the Old Testament seems to admit the existence of other gods — most famously in the Decalogue: "You shall have no other gods before me" (Ex. 20:3). Similarly, Exodus 23:32, "Do not make a covenant with them, or with their gods." Or what about Psalm 82:6, "[God] said, 'You are "gods"; you are all sons of the Most High.'"? The point is that the Old Testament is not a philosophical treatise, but practical theology. In fact, Israel was surrounded with peoples who believed in multiple gods. The text does not at the outset call the Israelites into a denial of the existence of other gods. It simply makes the remarkable demand that Israel shall not recognize any god but one. Soon enough in the text comes the categorical denial: "There is no god besides me" (Deut. 32:39), or "For all the gods of the nations are idols, but the LORD made the heavens" (Ps. 96:5). The point is that there is no place in the Old Testament where worship of any God but one is authorized. It may be argued when such an idea first appeared in Israel, but the text is uniform from end to end.

3. This is not to deny that at various points the idea of monotheism was to be found in other cultures (see the discussion of Greek philosophy above, e.g.). If monotheism is true, it would be surprising if that were not the case. But what is unique about the Bible is that it maintains monotheism as the only ruling principle throughout. It is not an idea to be considered from time to time along with other possibilities.

Iconoclasm

A second characteristic of Old Testament thought is iconoclasm: the insistence that God may not be represented in any created form. Once again the uniqueness of this idea must be stressed. How many iconoclastic religions are there in the world? Judaism, Christianity, and Islam — the same three that are monotheistic. And whence has come that iconoclasm in those three religions? It has come from the same single source from which monotheism derives: the Old Testament. Thus again, there is only one culture in the world where iconoclasm originated and was then maintained as a consistent principle.

Why should this be? On every side of Israel opulent religious practices centering on images were taking place. Yet Israel's prophets represent the worship of idols as perhaps the most basic departure from Israel's ancient faith. They act as though the denial of idolatry was at the very heart of Israel's understanding of reality. And what does that denial imply? Above everything else it implies that God is not to be identified with this world. There in the simple words of the second commandment, "You shall not make for yourself an image in the form of anything in heaven above or on the earth beneath or in the waters below. You shall not bow down to them or worship them" (Ex. 20:4 – 5a), is the germ of the doctrine of transcendence: God is not the world, cannot be identified with the world, and cannot be manipulated through the world. We can illustrate these ideas, however imperfectly, with the following diagram:

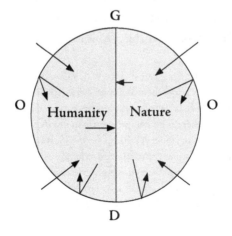

We might say that God "has made a space within himself" for the world and can penetrate it at will. Yet he ever remains distinct from his world. Thus, from our side there remains an impenetrable boundary between us and him (as there is between us and nature). Thus, all our attempts to manipulate him through the world are doomed to failure.

First Principle Is Spirit

A third characteristic of Old Testament thought is that the first principle is not matter but Spirit. Whatever one makes of the Hebrew grammar of Genesis 1:1, it is plain that God the Spirit is prior to everything.[4] If at the time he began to create the earth the matter he was working with was already in existence, there is not a hint of a suggestion that God the Spirit had proceeded from that matter. Rather, every indication is that he had brought that matter into existence. This is a startling viewpoint against the backdrop of the uniformity of all the rest of the religious statements of the ancient world. Furthermore, there is nothing in the Bible to suggest that chaotic matter is continually attempting to destroy an order forcibly imposed upon it by God. If there is chaos in the world, it is the result of rebellious created *spirits*.

Thus, the Bible avoids the tragic paradox of myth, namely, that matter is the basis of everything, but the matter that you and I encounter daily is finally transient and unreal because it is only a reflection of that invisible primal matter. The Bible goes in precisely the opposite direction: the Spirit is the basis of everything, but because he is the creator of matter it has a real and lasting significance. Thus the Bible is in a position to insist that the problem of humanity is not a tragic fatedness to evil, but a spirit that prefers evil to good.

---

4. Genesis 1:1 could be legitimately translated, "When God began to create the heavens and the earth, the earth without form and void" (cf. NEB and NRSV). But the KJV's "In the beginning God ..." reflects our earliest interpretation of the Old Testament as found in the Septuagint, and there is no compelling reason to depart from this (for the use of re'šit as an absolute noun, see Job 8:7; 42:12; Isa. 46:10). It is hard to avoid the conclusion that those who adopt the former translation do so because they think it demonstrates that at one time Hebrew thought presumed the preexistence of chaos. However, even if one does accept that translation, all that it actually says is what the traditional translation says, namely, God began to create with nothing, a formless void. It does not say that chaotic matter preexisted God.

If every other great world religion, except for those derived from the Old Testament, and modern science as well take it for granted that matter is the source of everything, why does the Old Testament take the opposite position? Must it not be that the Bible comes to a different conclusion because it starts with a different principle and reasons in a different direction?

Absence of Conflict in the Creation Process

The Old Testament's understanding of origins is very different from that found in Near Eastern myths. In the myths conflict is essential to the creative process.[5] Creation only emerged from the body of the Chaos Monster because victorious gods, with the slimmest of margins, defeated her. That is not the case in the Bible. Conflict may be a characteristic of the created cosmos, but that is not because conflict is a characteristic of reality. The world exists merely because God wants it to, not because of some cosmic struggle between the forces of order and the forces of disorder. Particularly in the world of modern Christianity, which perennially teeters on the verge of philosophical dualism, this point needs to be reiterated forcefully. Genesis 1 and 2 relate the story of the creation of the cosmos in an atmosphere of complete serenity. That matter was originally "without form and void" (*tohu wabohu* Gen. 1:2) says absolutely nothing about any resistance on the part of animated chaotic matter or about God's overcoming of the forces of evil in order to make the world. Struggle is a part of creation; it is not a part of ultimate reality.

Significantly, evil only enters the world through willful disobedience by human beings, and that well after creation is complete. God's responses in Genesis 3 are instructive. There is no sense in which he is threatened by Satan. In fact, he does not even address Satan as the cause of the event. He first deals with Adam and Eve and treats them as responsible and accountable. Only then does he speak to Satan, and that in an almost off-handed way, before he returns to address Adam and Eve.

This same motif continues throughout the Old Testament and into the New. Satan is not the equal of God and is no threat to God, and conflict

---

5. Although not all accounts include conflict to the same degree, it is only rare that conflict is not at the center of the process. See J. Walton, "Creation in Genesis 1:1 – 2:3 and the Ancient Near East: Order out of Disorder after Chaoskampf," *Calvin Theological Journal* 43 (2008): 48 – 63, for a discussion of these issues.

with him has nothing to do with the creative activity of God. This is especially clear in the opening chapters of the book of Job.[6] Against the backdrop of myth, this absence of conflict in the cosmic realm is nothing less than stunning. It argues that the biblical understanding of reality is not based on the assumption that ultimate reality and the present order of existence are continuous with each other.

Far from creation being the result of conflict between eternal principles of Order and Disorder, the Bible presents creation as being the result of the purposive will of God. God decides that something should come into existence, commands it to be so, and it is so. His repeated pronouncement on each of these phases of creation, "That's good," is what an artist says when his or her work corresponds to some previous plan in his or her mind. It is God's way of saying that the creation has conformed to what he had in mind when he began the process. This dual sense of purposefulness and serenity is further enhanced by the progressive order of the account in Genesis 1. There is an inescapable sense of development from general to specific or from simple to complex, a sense that is notably absent in the other creation accounts from around the world.

It is also worth noting that there is no sense in which creation is an emanation from God. In particular, the idea of creation by means of speech underlines this point. The cosmos is not the body of defeated chaos, as in the Babylonian story, nor is it the result of the sexual activity of the god or gods, as in several of the Egyptian accounts. Just as speaker and speech are separate entities, even though the speech came from the speaker, so creation and Creator are clearly separate from each other, and creation is a result of the purposeful activity of the Creator. Coupled with this is the idea that

---

6. It is to be wondered if Satan appears again at the end of the book in the guise of Behemoth and Leviathan. Leviathan is probably the name of one of the versions of the chaos monster in Canaanite mythology. Yet Job makes this supposedly cosmic being hardly more than a hapless crocodile. Is creation the result of some heaven-shaking conflict between Yahweh, the agent of good, and Satan-Leviathan, the agent of evil? Hardly!

    Another theme to be found in the book of Job is the so-called divine council, as the prologue recounts the coming of "the sons of God" before God. In the myths, the various gods come before the high god to convince him of their views and not infrequently win out over him. Is that the case here? Hardly, Yahweh takes counsel with no one and no one prevails on him (see a similar scene in 1 Kings 22:19 – 23). The Bible maintains that there are spirits who serve God, but not that they are of the same order of being as he.

is underlined in Isaiah: creation is a brand-new thing.[7] It is not something that is merely a reshaping of what has always been. This is something that simply did not exist before God spoke it into being.[8]

A High View of Humanity

Unlike the myths, the Bible shows a high view of humanity, and this is directly related to the biblical concept of origins. Instead of the gods being made in the image of humanity with all that seems to mean of determinism, pettiness, and materiality, humanity is made in the image of God with all that means of freedom, nobility, and personhood. But even when we say that, we must be clear that "image" as the Bible uses it does not involve some automatic partaking of the "stuff" of God. We are in his image because of free, divine choice. Because of that choice, we have the opportunity to participate with God in the development of earth's resources.

It is sometimes argued that Genesis 1 follows the same general order as the Babylonian myth about beginnings.[9] (Even this interpretation rests

---

7. See Isa. 48:7, where God insists that what he is doing at that time is a new "creation" that has not existed before. See also 45:18, where God says he did not create the earth as a chaos, but on purpose for inhabitation.

8. It is sometimes pointed out that in one of the Egyptian origin myths, the god Ptah speaks things into existence. Two things need to be said in that regard. First, as with monotheism, it is nowhere said in the Bible, nor am I saying, that the Bible is the only place where these ideas ever appeared. That is not what makes the Bible unique. What makes it unique is that it maintains these points of view exclusively and throughout. As was said above, in a pagan worldview it is entirely possible to maintain several contradictory views at once. But for some reason, the Bible does not do that, and it acts as if it is not possible. That one document somewhere once suggests that one way of thinking about origins is through the medium of speech is far from being "the same" as the Bible. Second, it is instructive to see what the Egyptian text actually says. It reads, "His Ennead [the Nine Gods] is before him in (in form of) teeth and lips. That is (the equivalent of) the semen and hand of Aturm. Whereas the Ennead of Atum came into being by his semen and his fingers, the Ennead (of Ptah), however, is the teeth and lips in this mouth, which pronounced the name of everything, from which Shu and Tefnut came forth, and which was the fashioner of the Ennead.... He is indeed Ta-tenen, who brought forth the gods, for everything came forth from him ..." (*ANET*, 5). This is not what is being said in Genesis. In fact it is simply an alternate way of expressing the idea that we exist as an emanation of the divine, something the Bible denies vehemently.

9. See E. A. Speiser, *Genesis* (Anchor Bible; Garden City, NY: Doubleday, 1964). For further discussion see below.

on an assumption about what appeared in a large lacuna near the end of the myth.) But even if we were to grant that assumption, still there are vast differences, and none so glaring as the significance given to humanity in the biblical account. To be sure, humanity is created last in the Babylonian account, as in the Bible. But here the similarity stops. In the Babylonian account humanity is an afterthought, brought into being from a combination of dust and the blood of one of the chaos monsters in order to provide the gods with food and adulation. In the Bible, humanity is created last because it is the apex of all that has gone before and because humans are to be given lordship over all the creation.

The same picture obtains in Genesis 2, where humanity is seen as the center of the circle of creation, playing the partner of God in giving the constitutive names to all that God has created. Some scholars deride these expressions as an instance of unbridled human arrogance. But that is not the point. If all the great world religions are in agreement that humanity in general, and human personality in particular, are of little significance in the great scheme of things, why does the Bible maintain the opposite exclusively and throughout?

Part of the significance of "the image of God" in humans relates to the significance of personality that is found in the Old Testament. Whatever else the Bible tells us about God, it shows us a full-orbed Person who is capable of interacting with his creation on any number of different levels. This is not a one- or two-dimensional mask to make intelligible or explicable the operation of mechanistic force. No, this is a Person who laughs and cries, who roars and croons, who loves and hates, who is frustrated and triumphant, who shows us that personality is not something accidental, to be downplayed as we seek the great commonalities of existence, but something at the very heart of existence itself. Both Spirit and personality are ultimate, not passing. This means that instead of our unique personalities being insignificant because they distinguish us from the impersonal All, they are of incredible significance because in that personality we are sharing in the unique personhood of the Creator.

The Reliability of God

But the Bible insists that if God is uniquely personal, he is yet absolutely consistent. He is determined to bless people even when it is not to his own advantage. This was what Jonah knew and it was what sent him away from Nineveh rather than toward it (Jon. 4:1 – 2). He reasoned that even the Assyrians might repent if they knew that their end was at hand, and he knew that God was so consistent that he would have mercy even on murderous Assyrians if there was the faintest reason to do so. In the event, all Jonah's fears were realized, and the Assyrians did repent and were spared.

Thus the word *hesed*, a word not attested outside Hebrew, comes to be used as the descriptor par excellence of God in the Old Testament. The word speaks of a completely undeserved kindness and generosity done by a person who is in a position of power. This was the Israelites' experience of God. He revealed himself to them when they were not looking for him, and he kept his covenant with them long after their persistent breaking of it had destroyed any reason for his continued keeping of it. Ultimately they came to understand that God's holiness, that which in common ancient Near Eastern terms separated a god from a human, was most to be seen in his character. Unlike humans, this deity was *not* fickle, undependable, self-serving, and grasping. Instead he was faithful, true, upright, and generous — always. So the typical description of him, found throughout the Old Testament, is that he is patient, slow to get angry, merciful, kind, and true. He is just in that he does not suspend cause and effect for his favorites. But he does limit those effects to three or four generations, whereas he extends the effects of obedience to thousands of generations.[10]

God Is Supra-Sexual

Another distinction between God and humans in the Bible is that God is not sexed. As a result, sexuality has nothing to do with ultimate reality in the biblical understanding. First of all, we note that creation is accomplished without any recourse to sexuality. In the myths, the gods come into existence through sexual means, reproduce themselves through their sexuality, and make a world that is reflective of their sexuality. In the Bible there is nothing of that sort. Gender and its accompanying sexual activity is an attribute of creation, but it plays no part at all in the production of creation.

This is so because the biblical God is supra-sexual. He is never said to have a consort; he never has intercourse with anyone; and he produces

---

10. See Ex. 34:6; Deut. 7:9, etc.

no divine or semidivine children. The New Testament, quite unlike the myths that would celebrate God's impregnating a virgin and getting a hero from her womb, is at great pains to avoid all those connotations. The Son is not God's child, some semidivine hero like Achilles, He is God himself in human flesh, produced not through a tryst between a virile god and a particularly desirable woman, but by the divine Spirit's overshadowing of a particularly virtuous maid.

We in the West have grown up with the idea that God is supra-sexual and so the idea is a commonplace to us, but the fact is, it is an incredible concept in its historical and cultural setting. Outside of Israel all gods or goddesses are sexed, and while there are myths where the sexuality of the deities is not the main feature, that characteristic is never far below the surface. The deities are either sexually male or sexually female and they function in those terms alone.

But it may be asked, "If God is supra-sexual, then why are exclusively male terms used of him?" The answer is fairly straightforward. The Hebrews wish to describe a God who, while he is not sexed, is yet fully personal. This means that even if the Hebrew language had neuter pronouns, which it does not, it would never stoop to describing God as an "it." The "Force" of Star Wars fame is not an advance in theological thinking — it is a precipitous decline.[11] This leaves three choices: exclusively male, exclusively female, or a mix of the two. The latter can be dismissed quickly. Contrary to some recent suggestions, androgyny is not a high theological concept; it is a physical monstrosity. To say that God is supra-sexual does not mean that God has both breasts and a penis. It means he has neither. He is not a reflection of creation. This means that to use terms of both genders to describe God can only lead to confusion.

We have now reduced the number of options for describing a personal deity who is not sexual to two: either exclusively male, or exclusively female. It is a fact of reality that male sexuality is concentrated almost wholly in penetration and ejaculation. It is a compartment in the male's life. It is direct and obvious, and can be all-consuming, but it is a compartment.

---

11. Note that this depersonaliztion of God is the inevitable result of the use of such abstract terms as Creator, Redeemer, and Sustainer to replace the supposedly objectionable Father, Son, and Holy Spirit.

Female sexuality is much more interior and diffuse. Ultimately, a woman's sexuality is inseparable from her being. Copulation is only one part, and often a minor part, of the expression of that sexuality. Much more significant to female sexuality is the lifelong process involving gestation and nurturing. As a result, it is much more difficult, if not impossible, to separate femaleness from sexuality. This does not make women inferior to men. In fact, from the point of view of the creation it makes them much more vital to the whole process. But it does mean that female terms are badly handicapped when it comes to their use to describe a God who is not sexed and from whose being creation does not emanate.

It is almost certainly as a result of these facts that goddesses all over the world are directly and inescapably linked to sexuality. Some gods are, but by no means all. This means that if you wish to tell of a deity who is fully personal but is other than sexual, the use of exclusively female terms is impossible. If you do use female terminology, you will end up where you started, whether you intend to or not. That is, you will subtly convey to yourself and to your hearers that, at heart, deity is profoundly sexual. If you use exclusively male terminology, you will still have to guard carefully against the sexual understanding creeping back in, but it will not be the virtually automatic connection that will occur if female terminology is used.

In my opinion, patriarchy, that obscene word of our times, has next to nothing to do with the use of male terminology for God. If it did, the sexual engendering function of the patriarch would be a central feature in the descriptions of God. Since that is not the case, we need not think that patriarchy is the reason for the phenomenon. Furthermore, if that were the case, there would be no patriarchy in those religions that recognize both gods and goddesses. But of course that is not the case; patriarchy was as much a part of those cultures as it was of Israelite culture.

On the other hand, the Fatherhood of God is far from being patriarchal in nature, as it is with the Canaanite El. Yahweh is not the male engenderer of a family, surrounded by a host of squabbling divine children alternately fawning on him and threatening him. Nor does his behavior authorize the sometimes outrageous behavior of the biblical patriarchs. Rather, Yahweh is a father in his roles and not in his sexual identity. He cares about his creatures in an intimate and personal way. He takes an interest in what interests them. He is moved with compassion for them. He relates to them in profoundly personal ways.

Sex Is Desacralized

Because God is not sexed and does not function in sexual ways, human sexual behavior is specifically desacralized. Nothing happens to God or to nature when a man and a woman have sex together. In fact, ritual prostitution is directly forbidden. We are not permitted to attempt to conceive of the universe in sexual terms, nor are we allowed to try to affect the universe's functioning through our sexual behavior. Sex is a divinely willed characteristic of creation, but it is not a characteristic of ultimate reality. As a result, the Bible builds specific boundaries around the practice of sex. It cannot be used as a way to join nature and humanity, or humanity and the divine. It is not to be used as a way of expressing our human limitlessness.

This is not an easy position to maintain because in every age, sex seems always to be waiting in the wings offering in itself unity with the divine, whether in power or in fulfillment. The myths around the world acquiesce in this, aiding and abetting the illusion. Only the Bible stands squarely against it. When we attempt to use our sexuality to scale the walls of heaven, it only drops us into hell. Used as God designed it, to be the deepest symbol of surrender, self-disclosure, and trust, all within the confines of unreserved commitment, it is a glorious thing. Used in any other way, sex will consume us. The biblical writers know this, and under God's inspiration they tell us there is only one place where we may freely express our sexuality: in the heterosexual marriage bed. Interestingly enough, in that setting the Bible places no restrictions on our sexual expression.

But it is suggested by some today that the restrictions against incest, homosexual practice, bestiality, and prostitution in all its forms are the work of some rural, patriarchal prudes. Is that true? Are the prohibitions of these behaviors merely the shocked reactions of the Israelite hayseeds at the freedoms of their liberated, cosmopolitan city cousins, the Canaanites? I think not. If that were the case, we should expect to find the same kinds of prohibitions among such people as the Edomites or the Moabites, even more rural than the Israelites. But there is no evidence of this being the case. And even more to the point, we should expect these quaint restrictions to drop quietly away as the Israelites themselves became more urbanized. If anything, however, the prophets are even more strident than the Pentateuch in their call for strict sexual faithfulness within the bounds of heterosexual marriage.[12]

No, the answer to our question must be sought elsewhere. The Hebrews take this unusual attitude towards sexuality because of their unusual understanding of God. If God is not sexed, then the use of sex to express and indeed, to reinforce, our unity with God is both mistaken and positively dangerous. We may believe most sincerely that the way to find real life is through the use of morphine, but the fact is that to use this drug in order to find satisfaction in life is the way to death. When it is used in controlled ways for medicinal purposes it is a positive blessing, deadening extreme pain so that the body can focus its energies on healing. But when the drug is used to find spiritual fulfillment, it always falls short of its initial promise and keeps beckoning us into deeper and deeper dependence until its end is death.

So it is with sex. If we use it to try to make ourselves gods, the end is destruction, because it cannot actually take us where it seems to point. God is beyond the limits of our sexuality. So, these prohibitions on sex outside of heterosexual marriage are not the work of prudes. They are a revelation of the boundaries inside of which the Creator intended us to find blessing and not curse.

Prohibition of Magic

Yet another example of these boundaries between God and creation is found in the prohibition of the use of all magic. Sorcery of every kind is forbidden, and the Israelites may not attempt to manipulate God in any kind of ritualistic way. Nowhere is this clearer than in the prophets with their insistence that the rituals in and of themselves accomplish nothing. It is only as the rituals express genuine repentance, exhibiting itself in the

---

12. Some will assert that the Hebrews did practice these kinds of behaviors more frequently as they became more urbanized, and that is the reason for the prophetic denunciations. But that is not the point. Why do these behaviors continue to be denounced? What was it in Israelite thought, contrary to that which was current all around Israel, that caused denunciation instead of at least acquiescence, and in many cases positive commands?

nonmanipulative behavior of righteousness and justice, that the ritual gives any pleasure to God at all. The attempt to lay hold of divine power to accomplish our purposes and to supply our own needs is represented as disgusting to God. He is not a part of this system and cannot be manipulated through it.

But if that is the case, how are the Israelites to get their needs supplied? They are to do so by surrendering themselves and their needs to God in trust and faith (Ps. 51:16 – 17). They are to do so through personal communication, that is, prayer.[13] This is, of course, a rather frightening alternative. As was said above, it is to put oneself at the mercy of the gods. But unlike the fickle gods, who sometimes bless their human worshipers but who also sometimes use those worshipers to aggrandize themselves, the biblical God is faithful, keeping his word no matter what the cost. He longs to bless his people if they will only surrender their own attempts to get what they want without commitment, and trust him. But the price of self-surrender is a high one, and we often find the Israelites slipping back into the attempts to manipulate God through magic.

This prohibition of magic calls our attention to a feature of the Israelite understanding of God that has been implicit in much that we have already observed. This is that Yahweh, the Holy One of Israel, is absolute. There is nothing and no one beyond him. There is no raw power, no "meta-divine" outside of him that can be appealed to through magic to force our will on him whether he likes it or not. Thus the Old Testament teaches us that the Absolute is a personal Spirit who is the source of all things — not because they emanate from him, but because of his creative will. He cannot be manipulated through the creation, but he intends to bless all those who will surrender their attempts to perform such manipulation.

Ethical Obedience as a Religious Response

Since we cannot relate to God in magical ways, how do we relate to him? Surprisingly, the Bible calls the Israelites to relate to him through

---

13. It is significant that in Solomon's dedicatory prayer for the temple (1 Kings 8), there is almost nothing said about sacrifice, but continual reference to it as a place for prayer and repentance. Note also that Isa. 56:7 (quoted by Jesus in Luke 19:46) refers to the temple as "a house of prayer for all nations."

ethical obedience. This is seen in the structure of the Sinai covenant. This is a religious document, detailing the terms of a relationship between a divine being and a people. What is religion about among the other cultures of the ancient Near East? It is about sacrifice, ritual, ritual purity, prayer, offerings, and the like. Those issues are certainly addressed in Yahweh's covenant with Israel, but they are hardly the only things addressed, and indeed are not the primary thing addressed. The Hebrews are told that the ways in which they treat their parents, their neighbors, their children, and the strangers among them are matters of intense religious concern. They show their commitment to their God by their commitment to tell the truth about each other, by the way in which they value one another's possessions, by the way they keep faith with their spouses, and so on.

The proportions of the Decalogue are significant at this point. The first four commandments may be said to address religious concerns, but the remaining six address social and civic ones. And these same proportions continue to prevail in the specific examples that follow in Exodus 21 – 23. The same is true in the restatement of the covenant in Deuteronomy. It is this feature that gives the Sinai covenant its great significance. Can analogues to many of the laws be found in the law codes mentioned above? Absolutely. And some are almost word for word the same.[14] But what makes the Old Testament unique is that these laws are given in the context of a covenant with God. Ethics are now no longer the province of the state because the king demands this of his followers. They are instead an expression of a committed relationship with a god.

And what is the basis of these ethical requirements? They are represented as being necessary because they are a reflection of the character of the God to whom the Israelites belong. Ethics are no longer merely a matter of civil and social concern. Here they are made a matter of cosmic concern.

Nowhere is this more clearly seen than in Leviticus 19, which can be seen as a brief summary of the covenant stipulations. It begins with a call for the Israelites to be holy as Yahweh is holy (v. 2). We might assume that this refers to some sort of cultic purity; but that is not the case. Immediately in

---

14. Most famously "The Law of the Goring Ox." See R. Yaron, "The Goring Ox in Near Eastern Laws," in *Jewish Law in Ancient and Modern Israel*, ed. H. Cohn (New York: KTAV, 1971), 50 – 60.

verse 3 we move to the first of the social commandments in the Decalogue: honoring of one's parents. Clearly the holiness being advocated here is not some cultic participation in the "Mysterium Tremendum," as Rudolph Otto labeled it.[15] To be holy as Yahweh is holy means to treat people as persons of value, not objects for one's own use. This ethical component of holiness is further developed throughout Leviticus 19, with the regular reminder that these requirements are incumbent on the people because "I am the LORD." That is, they must act in these ways because of their exclusive relationship with him and because of his distinctive ethical character.

What are the implications of all of this? If it is true that there is only one Creator of the universe, and if it is likewise true that the universe did not emanate from him but is an expression of his creative will, and if it is further true that the Creator is consistently ethical in his treatment of his creatures, then it becomes possible to say that there is but one ethical standard in the universe, one that reflects the ethical character of the Creator himself.[16]

The Importance of Human-Historical Activity

The ideas that God has created the world on purpose and that response to him is seen in obedience to him bring to the surface another important facet of the Israelite view of reality. Yehezkel Kaufmann expressed it in this way:

> The world was the domain of its one supreme God, yet within this domain there were still struggle and tension. This could no longer be interpreted mythically as the clash of divine forces. Instead, a new

---

15. Rudolf Otto, *The Idea of the Holy: An Inquiry into the Non-rational Factor in the Idea of the Divine and its Relation to the Rational*, trans. J. Harvey (London: Oxford, 1926).

16. On the destructive impact of the worldview of continuity upon a sense of ethical responsibility, here is John Calvin: "As soon as that error prevails, that the life of man is governed by the influence of the stars, the judgment-seat of God is overthrown, so that he is not the judge of the world in inflicting punishments, or in restoring to life by his mercy those who were perishing. They who think that the stars, by their irresistible influence control the life of men, immediately become hardened to the imagination of destiny, so that they leave nothing to God" (*Commentary on Isaiah*, trans. W. Pringle [Grand Rapids: Eerdmans, 1948], 387).

dimension was being called into being, the historical-moral; expressed in the saga of man's defiance of God. History was conceived as a struggle between the will of God and man.[17]

What this means is that if the human experience is to be correctly understood, it is human behavior in creation in relation to God that must be studied and not the relations of the gods among themselves in primeval time. This study is made even more important in the light of the biblical insistence that human behavior is not predetermined through continuity. Humans are free to make decisions that actually defy the will of the Creator. To be sure there will be tragic effects of such decisions, but they will be the result of divine justice and not the result of magical continuities between forces.

Suddenly it becomes important to know why a person made the decisions they did and what were the effects of such decisions. Why? Because that is where God is known: in the human-historical world of ethical choice. He is not to be known through metaphysical speculation resting on the assumption that he is continuous with the cosmos. He is *not* the cosmos, but he breaks into it, revealing his purposes to us and calling us to decide for or against those purposes. William Hallo, professor emeritus of ancient Near Eastern studies at Yale University, points up the distinction in the two ways of thinking by contrasting the omens of the surrounding cultures with the Hebrew prophets. He notes that both served the same function: guides to behavior. But there, he says, the similarities cease.

> The contrast [of omen texts] with biblical prophecy could not be greater. There [in biblical prophecy] an immutable divine dispensation, but free will on humanity's part to avoid divine displeasure. Here [in omens] is a wholly capricious pantheon largely indifferent to human behavior and to be appeased rather by elaborate and costly cultic behavior.[18]

---

17. Y. Kaufmann, *The Religion of Israel*, trans. M. Greenberg (Chicago: Univ. of Chicago Press, 1960), 240. H. Frankfort recognizes the same thing when he says (using what I believe is an inadequate definition of myth), that the Israelites replaced the nature myths of their neighbors with the myth of the will of God; see his *Before Philosophy* (Baltimore: Pelican, 1964), 244.

18. W. Hallo, *The Book of the People* (Atlanta: Scholars, 1991), 31.

For the first time in human experience it becomes vitally important to record unique activities of individual humans in time and space, especially those in which the humans made unique decisions. For it is in those instances, and not in the great recurrences of nature, that the personal God is to be most truly known.

One of the features of the records of human behavior found in the Old Testament is that God is goal-oriented. At the outset three of his purposes for humans were frustrated as a result of their willful disobedience. Those purposes were: undisturbed fellowship between humans and himself; the reproduction of his character in them; and their harmony with the creation (Gen. 1 – 3). Genesis 4 – 11 detail those effects and their spiraling manifestations in the world. But even in those chapters we see God's unwillingness to give up the human race and the first intimations of his absolute determination to bless humans wherever he can.

In Genesis 12 we see the beginnings of God's attempt to reinstate humanity in his plan of blessing. That start is small. All it is, is a series of promises to supply elemental human wants to a couple named Abram and Sarai. But in this small start is the germ of large things. The promises are not immediate. If they are to be fully realized a long time will need to elapse, and during that time Abram and Sarai and their descendants will need to cultivate a long-term habit of obedience and faith. In other words, the fact that God has long-term goals for humans and that the realization or nonrealization of those goals will be dependent on patterns of human behavior over a long span of time invites, nay, requires the keeping of careful records of that behavior if God is to be known at all. Nothing like this is to be found in the myths or in the surrounding cultures.[19]

What I have attempted to demonstrate in the previous paragraphs is that on all the central points that characterize the thought world of myth, the Bible differs, not merely somewhat but diametrically. This means that it is not appropriate to call the Bible myth. This is not to say that the Bible

---

19. This is not to say that the other religious literatures of the ancient Near East do not see their gods as acting in history. They do, as was demonstrated clearly by B. Albrektson, *History and the Gods: An Essay on the Idea of Historical Events in the Ancient Near East and in Israel* (Lund: Gleerup, 1967). But these tend to be isolated occurrences and are far from the settled and consistent approach of promise and fulfillment found in the Old Testament. See below in chapter 7 for further discussion.

is necessarily true. Conceivably, its ideas could be wrong, as those who advocate a return to paganism today maintain. But it is still not myth. To be sure, it is literature about the supernatural. But it upholds a completely different understanding of the supernatural than we find in myth. To blur that difference by using a definition of myth that is so broad as to be meaningless is to do a disservice to the search for truth and understanding.

TRANSCENDENCE AS THE UNDERLYING PRINCIPLE

What is the common denominator in all these facets of the biblical understanding of reality? Above everything else it is the principle of God's relation to the cosmos. In mythical thinking God *is* the cosmos — or, to put it the other way around, the cosmos is God. The Source and the Manifestation are finally indistinguishable. As we saw in the previous chapter, all the distinctive features of mythical thought flow from this principle, the principle we called continuity.

In the same way all of the Bible's understandings stem from one ruling principle: it is the principle of transcendence. For the Bible, God is not the cosmos, and the cosmos is not God. God is radically other than his creation. This thought undergirds everything the Bible says about reality. From start to finish, the Bible adamantly resists the principle of continuity. God and the divine realm are not in any way a part of this world. He is everywhere present *in* the world, but He is *not* the world and the world is *not* Him. He is other than the world; He is separate from it; it does not proceed from him as a somewhat blurred reflection; it is a creation that, by his permission, has a distinct existence from his own. This is the law of transcendence, and it means that God is wholly other than the cosmos.

It is this underlying conviction of transcendence that explains how Israel could maintain monotheism when all the brilliant peoples around Israel insisted on polytheism. I have argued elsewhere that Egyptian religion was headed in a monotheistic direction during the last years of the second millennium BC.[20] But not having a philosophical principle to support

---

20. John Oswalt, *The Concept of Amon-Re as Reflected in the Hymns and Prayers of the Rameside Period* (Ann Arbor, MI: University Microfilms, 1968).

that thrust, they could not maintain it and fell back into the grossest polytheism. The same was true in Greece between 625 and 325 B.C. But unless there is an underlying change in the understanding of reality, these intuitions are unsustainable. Continuity simply makes monotheism impossible, while transcendence does make it possible, and indeed, requires it. Only one being can truly transcend all other beings.

The same thing is true for iconoclasm. The Israelites are forbidden to make an image of God because that would immediately suggest that God is a part of this world and can be manipulated through this world. This is why Moses became so violently angry when he saw the people worshiping their old fertility symbol from Egypt, the bull (Ex. 32:19 – 20). It was not merely because they had broken their covenant commitment to God as expressed in the second commandment, but that they were headed down a road that would lead them directly back into the theological darkness from which God was seeking to deliver them. Continuity thinking may maintain that the divine is not the world and is the world at the same time, but in the end that faulty logic can no better support life than it can support thought. Moses understood that and knew that if transcendence was ever to be maintained, it was going to require a radical denial of God's continuity with the world in any form; hence the drastic measures he took.

Likewise, transcendence explains Israel's unique insistence that sexuality has no place in worship and that it can only be practiced within specific limitations. Transcendence means that there are boundaries between the realms, boundaries that make it impossible for human beings to manipulate either deity or nature through magical transference. The Bible's placing of rigid boundaries on the practice of sex is one outgrowth of the principle.

Why did the doctrine of transcendence only find rootage among one people, and a rather insignificant people (by their own witness) at that? Why has the doctrine of continuity reigned supreme around the world? Is it because transcendence is so philosophically abstruse? No, it is because continuity is much more comfortable. Transcendence means that there is no way in which I can mechanically manipulate the forces that ultimately control my life. This is what Paul is talking about in Romans 1. To give God the glory due him (1:21) is to admit his transcendence, to admit that I and my desires are not God. That admission is too costly for most of us. In order to make God in our image, we would rather submit to all the inevitable results of continuity.

This is what happened with Aristotelian thought. By the application of rigorous logic, Aristotle arrived at the conclusion that there must be One behind everything. But his logic was so rigorous that he could not conceive of any way in which the One could relate to what it had set in motion without diminishing Itself. So he called the One the "Unmoved Mover." Unlike the Old Testament God, who could not be manipulated but who did wish to bless humans, the "Unmoved Mover" was completely untouched by human need. It is not hard to understand why Aristotle's thought had almost no impact on the practice of Greek religion. If the purpose of religion is to make divine power accessible to humans, and if the most satisfactory way of doing that (to the fallen human mind) is by means of continuity thinking, such ideas as Aristotle's were useless. As a result, the profusion of Greek gods only became more lush as the years passed.

It is common for critics of the position I am representing here to point out that there may never have been a time when the Israelite people believed or practiced these ideas exclusively. That is certainly true, on the Bible's own witness. As I have just said, the alternative to transcendence has never lost its appeal. So it should not be surprising if, at the same moment Moses is receiving the Decalogue on the mountain, the people of Israel are dancing around a golden calf in the valley below. Similarly, it should come as no surprise that the Israelites did not want to worship God in one place only. Neither should we be shocked to find that many Israelites wanted to engage in ritual prostitution and child sacrifice.

But none of this changes the reality of the text! Nowhere *in the text* is God said to be many; nowhere *in the text* is God identified with this world; nowhere *in the text* is God said to function in sexual ways, nor is it permissible anywhere *in the text* to worship him in sexual ways. This is the point. Alone in the ancient world the Old Testament insists throughout on a way of thinking about reality that is unique. It will not do to say that the Egyptian Pharaoh Akhenaton was a sort of a monotheist in the fourteenth century BC. That is an aberration, a bubble on an otherwise untroubled sea of polytheism in Egypt before and after him. So it is with other proposed isolated similarities that appear from time to time in the surrounding cultures. If the biblical worldview is true, we should be surprised *not* to find such instances. The point is that the Bible is absolutely thoroughgoing in its opposition to everything going on around Israel. That cannot be gainsaid.

Neither will it do to say that this philosophical unity was imposed on the text late in the postexilic period. Even if we were to grant this dubious proposal, we would still have to answer the question: How did this total worldview come to be imposed? Are we to think that the Israelite litera-ture had been continuity-based and thus polytheistic, fertility-saturated, antihistorical, and idolatry-filled prior to the exile, and then that during the chaotic four hundred years between the return from the exile and the appearance of the Dead Sea Scrolls (ca. 150 BC) when the community was badly fractured with political and religious hatreds growing up on every side, that some group succeeded in tearing the literature right loose from its roots and transforming it absolutely so that no trace of support for continu-ity thought remains?[21] I submit that that is to ask far too much. If we are to understand where this thoroughgoing commitment to transcendence and all its implications comes from, we must think again.

---

21. This is the position of William Dever in his *Did Yahweh Have a Wife? Archaeology and Folk Religion in Ancient Israel* (Grand Rapids: Eerdmans, 2005). He argues that during the late divided monarchy an elite group of priests and prophets emerged in Judah who objected to the continuity-based Israelite religion up to that time. One of the things that motivated them was misogyny. They were able to use the Babylonian conquest to their advantage and emerged from the chaos of the exile as the only group "still on their feet." Through skillful maneuvering they were able to force their agenda on the other disorga-nized religious groups among the returned exiles. Even if one were to grant the possibility of this tenuous proposal, the argument above stands: it is not reasonable to believe that this small group could be successful in totally altering the worldview of the entire Israelite literature. See chapter 9 for further discussion.

CHAPTER 5

THE BIBLE VERSUS MYTH

To this point I have argued that the Bible is essentially different from the religious literatures of the ancient Near East, and indeed, of the rest of the world. I have maintained that the thought world of the Bible is so radically different from that of the others that the similarities that undoubtedly do exist between the Bible and the others are superficial and not essential. In this chapter I wish to explore these issues further. I will show that the similarities do not indicate unity with the thought world around Israel but are the result of cultural adaptation, using readily available forms and terms to say something quite new.

ETHICS

Ethics in the Nonbiblical Ancient Near East

We will begin at a point touched on in the previous chapter, that of ethics and religion. In the thought world of continuity, ethical misbehavior is primarily of two sorts. There are offenses against the gods and there are offenses against other human beings. These two are of quite different natures. Offenses against the gods are almost entirely in the cultic or magical realms. Some magical taboo is violated or a divine prerogative is usurped. For instance, in the Gilgamesh epic, the goddess Ishtar becomes obsessed with the hero Gilgamesh and wishes to marry him. But he refuses, saying that she devours her lovers.[1] There is, of course, a great deal of wisdom here for heroes of any time. The sex goddess will come fawning upon

---

1. See *The Context of Scripture: Canonical Compositions, Monumental Inscriptions, and Archival Documents from the Biblical World*, ed. W. Hallo and K. L. Younger, 3 vols. (New York: Brill, 1997 – 2002), 458 – 61. Hereafter COS.

him, offering free love. The wise man will know enough to refuse her blandishments, realizing that what she really offers is an addiction that must eventually become an insatiable craving (see Prov. 9:13 – 18).

But Ishtar is not so easily put off; she presses her case more and more furiously until during a final exploit of daring, when Gilgamesh and his bosom friend Enkidu have killed the Bull of Heaven, Enkidu tears off a leg of the Bull and throws it in Ishtar's face, a terrible insult. That offense is too much; Enkidu has gone too far and must die. He has not disobeyed a divine command, nor has he injured anyone in any way. But he has angered the goddess by insulting her.

The offense against humans is of a different sort. Here the crime is against the customary regulations of society. The pattern of these is best known from several examples of law codes that have been unearthed in Mesopotamia. These laws are stated as cases: that is, if such and such an offense is committed, then such and such a punishment is to be meted out. Typically, the codes are said to have been authorized by a god. In Hammurapi of Babylon's case, it is Shamash, the sun god, who is said to give Hammurapi the right to dispense beneficence and order. But the laws themselves are understood to be human creations. Thus, the judgments in the cases are never derived from an appeal to any divine principles, nor are divine sanctions introduced after the opening words of divine authorization. Evidently what this means is that the law codes are a compilation of precedents from within the culture. This in turn means that there is no consistent rationale for ethical behavior on the earthly plane. Offenses against the gods have nothing to do with our treatment of each other, and offenses against humans are judged solely on the basis of the customary behavior of a culture.[2]

Given the characteristics of the mythical worldview, all this is highly consistent. It is not possible to talk of overarching principles of behavior on any specific level, because the universe is without purpose and has no one divine being who has the authority to say, "This is the way you were made; you must live in these ways." Furthermore, how humans treat each

---

2. For a discussion, see J. Walton, *Ancient Near Eastern Thought and the Old Testament: Introducing the Conceptual World of the Hebrew Bible* (Grand Rapids: Baker, 2006), 295 – 96.

other has no final cosmic significance. This world is but a reflection of the invisible real world, and our actions are only reflections of heavenly activities. We may be punished for what we have done, but that does not mean that we originated the deed. If that seems unfair, it is simply part of the bad joke of being a human being. As a result, it does not pay to spend a lot of time trying to understand why someone did something, or trying to change one's behavior. We simply try to deal with the results and go on around the wheel.

Ethics in the Bible

Beneath a number of superficial similarities that we will discuss below, there is in the Bible a completely different approach to ethics. Yes, there are cultic sins. Nadab and Abihu casually bring a different kind of fire into the sanctuary than that which had just been commanded of them, and they die (Lev. 10:1 – 2).[3] Likewise, there is customary or case law, in which a certain punishment is prescribed for a specific offense (e.g., Ex. 21:1 – 22:16). Many of these case laws are similar, or even in a few cases, identical to those found in the Mesopotamian law codes. Furthermore, as with the Mesopotamian codes, the law is introduced as having been given by God (Ex. 20:1). But the biblical statements about ethics are put in a completely different context than are those of their neighbors, and this different context in the end gives us a much different understanding of the significance of ethical behavior.

As I said in the previous chapter, that different context is covenant. God's people are to understand their whole lives not as fated reflections of heavenly causes, but as chosen responses to divine initiatives here on earth, because that is what a covenant is. The importance of the appropriation of this concept can hardly be overstated. No longer do the Hebrews do what they do because society requires it. Now they make their decisions about ethical questions on the basis of their exclusive relationship with the one God.

As some readers will know, the form of the covenant between God and the Israelites seems to have been adapted from the form of certain political

---

3. But it should be noted that this is a transgression of a specific commandment and not an unconscious offense, as is often the case in the myths.

treaties in the ancient Near East. How closely it duplicates this form and whether it is the form of an earlier or a later period is a matter of scholarly debate, but that it is essentially the same form is now widely accepted. It is the form of the agreement between a great king and a subject people. Among other things such a treaty spelled out the actions of the king that led up to the signing of the agreement. It also contained a statement of what the king would do for the people and a list of the things that the king demanded of the people in the light of their relationship to him. It is noteworthy that these demands often contained absolute prohibitions. These were not case-by-case statements of customary law, but rather, across-the-board prohibitions based on the king's wishes and desires.[4]

Why was such a form used to express the relationship between Yahweh and Israel? Since the Bible does not explicitly answer that question, any answer I give here must be speculative. But I think the answer is directly related to the conflict between transcendence and continuity. All of the prevailing religious forms of the day were irrecoverably wedded to continuity with its concomitant polytheism, idolatry, fertility, ethical relativism, and the like. Furthermore, nothing in the religious literature of the region provided a means of expressing the idea that a god or goddess would commit himself or herself irrevocably to a people. Thus it was necessary to go right outside that literature to find a way to communicate an idea of God that was different from the prevailing idea everywhere else.

What the covenant form means for the Israelite understanding of ethics is, first of all, that ethics become wholistic. No longer is cultic sin in relation to the god while social sin is in relation to the community. In the Mosaic covenant the entire gamut of behavior, whether cultic, social, or personal, is seen as an expression of either obedience or disobedience to God. So persons are required to remain ceremonially clean as a part of their covenant obedience to God. But they are also required to honor their parents and not to steal as a part of the same covenant obedience. Thus, how an Israelite treats other people is as religiously significant as whether he or she is ceremonially clean.

---

4. For a helpful discussion of this form and its implications, see Kenneth A. Kitchen, *On the Reliability of the Old Testament* (Grand Rapids: Eerdmans, 2003), 283 – 307.

In fact, a review of the punishments for the two types of offenses shows that treatment of other people is frequently more significant to God than ceremonial cleanness. In this respect it is significant that the cultic, social, and personal laws are rather thoroughly mixed together in the Torah. Leviticus 19 was mentioned in the previous chapter; it is a "parade" example of this mixing. The point is that all of the covenant stipulations have the same basis — love for God — so they are not to be separated from each other (see especially Deut. 10:12 – 11:1).

Second, the placing of ethical requirements within the context of a covenant with God means that there is a single standard against which all behavior may be judged. That standard is the character of the one God, the covenant Lord, to whom the people were responsible. The stipulations of the political covenants expressed the character of the kings who were making them. In the same way the biblical covenant expressed the character of God. When the idea that there is only *one* God is coupled with the idea that he is the sole creator of the universe, one soon realizes that these standards are expressive of the very nature of the universe.

So long as there is a multiplicity of gods, it is impossible to believe that the universe is profoundly ethical. Each god has different wishes and desires, often conflicting with those of others. An exclusive attempt to please one would almost certainly produce behavior that would offend another god. So the best policy is not to become too radical in obedience to any set of principles. Beyond that, since no one god originated the universe, then no one god's character is reflected in it. Its principles and character are more diverse than can be imagined, far too complex for anyone to spend a lot of time trying to understand. Ethical relativism is not merely a possibility in a world of continuity but a necessity. In a world of transcendence as the Bible has defined it, however, there can be only one standard of ethics, namely, the character of the Creator. Given the impossibility of relating to this transcendent One in magical or ritualistic ways, it is primarily in ethical behavior reflecting his character that we best express a correct relationship with him.

The third implication of the covenant form for ethics is that there is a traceable chain of cause and effect. The form sets out clear expectations for the performance of the parties to the covenant. Furthermore, there are stated, clear results that will follow from compliance or noncompliance with these expectations. By placing the entire world of divine-human relations within the setting of the covenant, God has made it plain that the same kinds of causes and effects that apply in the physical world apply in the world of ethics and morality as well.

In the world of continuity that is not true. Because the divine world mirrors the visible world, cause and effect is basically mechanical. The log falling on my leg is as likely to break the leg if I am an honest man as if I am a liar. Thus, ethics have little to do with causation in the physical world. So, reasoning that the invisible world is analogous with the visible world, the same must be true in the divine realm; ethics have little to do with ultimate causation. Also, since the gods are human beings written large, they are only as ethical as we are. This means that ethical behavior on the part of a human being may be significant for practical social relations, but that significance is strictly pragmatic. Ethics are of relatively little importance in understanding and evaluating human behavior. This is, of course, amplified by the belief that all human choices are fated anyway.

For the Hebrews, believing that ethical choices are the primary way in which humans can relate to the transcendent God, the possibility of tracing the impact of these choices became important. It was important theologically, because it became possible to gain deeper insight into God's nature by studying how he reacted when humans did certain things either in compliance with, or in defiance of, his commands. No longer was reality to be explained by references to direct ontological continuities between realms. Transcendence had broken that. Instead, reality was to be known through the ways in which the spiritual, personal God dealt with people who made certain choices with respect to His will. No longer was the effect the result of some unknown activity in heaven. Now the effect was understood to be the predictable outcome of some human's choice with regard to a known standard of behavior that was written into the very nature of things. The implications of this understanding for the way in which records were kept is of vast importance and we will give it more attention below.

The fourth implication of the confluence of the principle of transcendence and the covenant form is human freedom and the reality of choice. Once the idea of continuity is broken, determinism, though still possible, is not necessary. Our choices are not automatically reflective of cosmic events.

That the earthly Jerusalem fell does not mean that the forces of chaos have finally defeated the Lord on the heavenly stage. In fact, there is no such stage, or if there is, it is utterly different from anything we could imagine and its activities in no way precondition what takes place here. No, the sole reason Jerusalem fell was because its inhabitants made a series of human choices. They chose to oppress the poor, adulate the mighty, amass great wealth, falsify their weights and measures (not to mention their accounts), deify their sexuality, and seek their security in the forces of nature which had been given human-like faces and called gods. That is, they broke their covenant with God. This reason, and no other, shout the prophets, is why Jerusalem fell, and Samaria before it. Human choices, freely made, have observable effects, and the relationship between cause and effect is clearly traceable.

The Significance of Similarities between Israelites and non-Israelites

Similarities in Practice

Now what about similarities and differences? Without any question, there are some significant similarities between the practices of the Hebrews and the practices of the neighboring peoples. The Mesopotamians have law codes, and so do the Hebrews. In fact, some of the laws, as has already been noted, are virtually identical. The sacrificial practices of the Hebrews and their concern for ceremonial cleanness are often similar to what we know of these among the surrounding peoples. The structure of the covenant comes straight out of the ancient Near Eastern world.

There is now some evidence that the Hebrews may not have been the first ones to conceive of their relationship with their God in covenant terms of some sort. The kinds of sacrifices and the manner of their offering, as dictated in Leviticus, can be paralleled in a number of places elsewhere in the ancient world. The layout of the tabernacle and of the temple following it is essentially the same as the layout of contemporary Canaanite sanctuaries.[5] Furthermore, the decoration of the temple seems to have been similar

---

5. Kitchen has argued that the idea of a moveable sanctuary was derived from Egyptian prototypes (ibid., 275–83).

to that of the Canaanite sanctuaries. In the light of these kinds of evidence, should we not say that Hebrew religion is just a variant of the general west Semitic religion of its day?

We should not, because these similarities are not the key issues when it comes to describing Hebrew belief. What is significant is the way in which the Israelites utilize these features in a belief system that is radically different from anything around them. Again I want to stress that what is significant about Israelite religion is not that some unique idea appears, but that the whole way of thinking about reality is unique and that it is absolutely thoroughgoing in the Bible. It is not significant whether Akhenaton was a monotheist or not. What is significant is that Egyptian culture abandoned this idea with alacrity as soon as the king was dead. In the same way, it is not significant that the Mesopotamians had law codes, or that they claimed they got them from a god. What is significant is that they could not maintain the idea that not stealing from one's neighbor is an expression of obedience to the Creator. It is not significant that the Israelite worship center was tripartite, like the Canaanite ones, but that there was no idol in the innermost room.

What is significant about the Israelite religion is the way it puts these components together and what it draws from them when they are put together. We should not be at all surprised if the Israelite culture shows similarities with those around it. It would be much more shocking if there were no such similarities. The insistence that something must be absolutely different before we will admit a *fundamental* difference is unrealistic. So the issue is not whether some of the components in a pattern are the same as those found in another pattern. The discovery of such similar components says nothing about the similarity of the final patterns. And it is in the final patterns that the differences between the Hebrew and the ancient Near Eastern approach to ethics are unmistakable.

Is the form of the Hebrew covenant similar to the form of the Hittite suzerainty covenants? Certainly. Are many of the laws of the Torah similar to those found in law codes elsewhere? Yes. But those similarities are not the issue. What is at issue is what happens when a law code is put inside a covenant with a transcendent God. The result is something unique. Nowhere else is ethical behavior regularly and consistently made the mark of the quality of one's relationship to God. Nowhere else is there an absolute system of ethics. Nowhere else is one's ritual behavior made less significant than one's treatment of others in evaluating the quality of their relationship with God, so much so that one's ritual behavior is invalidated by a lack of justice and right dealing (see Amos 5:21 – 27, etc.). And these are not simply "sports," aberrations that suddenly jut up and then equally suddenly disappear. Rather, these are the consistent pattern of Old Testament understanding from Genesis to Malachi.

Similarities in Expression

But apart from covenant and law code, are there not other more serious similarities that call into question my assertions concerning the remarkable contrast between the worldview of the Old Testament and the worldview of myth? While I do not think these others *are* more serious, they do exist, and we must turn to look at them now.

The first objection to the position I have taken is that the Bible does not in fact radically reject the thought world of myth because it employs some of the actual ancient Near Eastern myths to express itself. The most common of these is the story that a god defeated the chaos monster in primeval time and so brought order into the world. This monster was called Leviathan in Canaanite literature. In Mesopotamia, chaos was known as Tiamat. In Egypt it was called Nun, although from certain biblical references, it appears that the name Rahab might also have been used.

The basic assertion is correct; references to one or another form of these stories do appear in several places in the Bible. The most explicit examples are found in Job 41:1 – 11; Psalm 74:12 – 17; Isaiah 51:9 – 10; see also Habakkuk 3:8 – 11. But the issue is not that they occur; rather, how are they used? That you might call someone a Hercules does not prove that your view of the world is the same as that of the ancient Greeks from whose myths that personage comes. And in fact, the Bible's usages are directly analogous to that example. What we have is a self-conscious appropriation of the language of myth for historical and literary purposes, not mythical ones.

For instance, Leviathan in Job is not depicted as some primeval monster who threatens God and all ordered existence. Instead, he is depicted in very this-worldly terms — so much so that commentators have debated whether anything more than a crocodile is intended. I suspect that the use of the Canaanite name does indicate that the writer wants to convey something more. But he is using the material in a quite different way than the Canaanites did. God is simply asking Job in another way the question which he has put to him several times, "Can you control nature?" In this case he uses a common literary figure from Job's world to convey the might of nature, but nothing more. In no way is the worldview of continuity presupposed here. It is not suggested that Leviathan precedes Yahweh or that Yahweh emerged from Leviathan. Neither is it suggested that Leviathan is in any way a threat to Yahweh. In fact, as the story is told, Yahweh's absolute sovereignty is only underlined.[6]

Leviathan and Rahab are used in a different way in the other three places:

But God is my king from long ago;
    he brings salvation on the earth.
It was you who split open the sea by your power;
    you broke the heads of the monster in the waters.
It was you who crushed the heads of Leviathan
    and gave it as food to the creatures of the desert.
It was you who opened up springs and streams;
    you dried up the ever-flowing rivers.
The day is yours, and yours also the night;
    you established the sun and moon.
It was you who set all the boundaries of the earth;
    you made both summer and winter. (Ps. 74:12 – 17)

Awake, awake, arm of the LORD,
    clothe yourself with strength!
Awake, as in days gone by,
    as in generations of old.
Was it not you who cut Rahab to pieces,
    who pierced that monster through?

---

6. For another interpretation of this material, see N. Wyatt, "'Water, Water, Everywhere …': Musings on the Aqueous Myths of the Near East," in *The Mythic Mind* (London: Equinox, 2005), 189 – 237.

Was it not you who dried up the sea,
　　the waters of the great deep,
who made a road in the depths of the sea
　　so that the redeemed might cross over? (Isa. 51:9 – 10)

Were you angry with the rivers, LORD?[7]
　　Was your wrath against the streams?
Did you rage against the sea
　　when you rode your horses
　　and your chariots to victory?
You uncovered your bow,
　　you called for many arrows.
You split the earth with rivers;
　　the mountains saw you and writhed.
Torrents of water swept by;
　　the deep roared
　　and lifted its waves on high.
Sun and moon stood still in the heavens
　　at the glint of your flying arrows,
　　at the lightning of your flashing spear.
In wrath you strode through the earth
　　and in anger you threshed the nations.
You came out to deliver your people,
　　to save your anointed one.
You crushed the leader of the land of wickedness,
　　you stripped him from head to foot.
With his own spear you pierced his head
　　when his warriors stormed out to scatter us,
gloating as though about to devour
　　the wretched who were in hiding.
You trampled the sea with your horses,
　　churning the great waters. (Hab. 3:8 – 15)

In each of these passages it is the exodus that is in view. Here the imagery is utilized to express God's victory over evil when he triumphed over

---

7.　In Canaanite myths, another name for the chaos monster is "River."

the waters in the exodus and brought his people through. The fact that chaos was considered to be the watery deep makes it especially adaptable for this use to refer to God's deliverance through the sea. But the point is that God's victory over chaos does not occur continuously in the primeval realm. Rather, he conquered the chaos of evil once for all for his people at a certain time and in a certain place.

This kind of appropriation of the figures is diametrically opposite to their original use among the pagans. Here we have no primeval struggle between the forces of light and darkness. Here the transcendent God is accomplishing his will through an obedient nature in a specific historic event. In a unique moment in time and space, never to be repeated, but also never to be forgotten, God has worked redemption for his people. Nothing is conditioned by that event, but people are called to make their choices and order their lives, real possibilities, in the light of that event. This is anything but mythical thinking. The figures are being used in a literary way, not a philosophical one. As Brevard Childs has said, the Hebrew understanding of existence is so distinctive that it can only utilize myth by "breaking it."[8]

Beyond these and three or four briefer allusions of the same sort, there are no other references to specific myths in the Bible. This is remarkable given the fact that Israel was completely surrounded by myths and mythical thinking. Furthermore, it is noteworthy to observe where in the biblical corpus these references appear. They are late in Israelite history. It is as though the worldview of transcendence has sufficiently matured and has become enough engrained that now the imagery of the mythical literature can be self-consciously appropriated for another whole set of purposes, a set of purposes contrary to that which was intended by the mythmakers. If we take the point of view that these are holdovers from an earlier stage of Israelite religion, then it seems to me that we are hard-pressed to explain what they are doing in these few places. Why were they not expunged with all the rest of the supposed original uses? Why leave these few, and only these? It seems much more likely to me that a conscious appropriation of literary imagery is the better explanation.

---

8. B. Childs, *Myth and Reality in the Old Testament*, 2nd ed. (London: SCM, 1962), 72.

Similarities in Thought Patterns

However, some would say that the specific use of the language of myth in certain places in the Bible is not the issue. Rather, they would argue, much stronger evidence is to be found in the first chapters of Genesis, where they maintain there is evidence of dependence on mythical thought patterns. While no precise borrowing is alleged to have taken place, nevertheless it is said that the evidence shows there was an original Hebrew myth that partook of the same general ground forms as the rest of the ancient world.[9] For some reason, later Israel broke away from this kind of thinking, but Genesis shows that Israel started where everyone else did.

I have earlier argued that such an idea does not make sense. If Israel and her neighbors all started with the worldview of continuity, then others besides Israel should have broken away from it. Yet she alone did. And if Israel broke away, when did that take place? Those who espouse such an idea offer a plethora of different suggestions, ranging from the early monarchy to the postexilic period. And what caused the breaking away? Here there is even more uncertainty and tentativeness. Surely it must have been something of a fundamental nature to have caused Israel to abandon the understanding of reality to which everyone else agreed; yet no one seems to know what that something was.[10]

From my perspective, the biblical facts cannot be accounted for by some gradual evolutionary growth away from an original base in mythical thinking. The fact that the entire Bible as it now stands is written from the perspective of the transcendent God breaking into human history and revealing himself through unique events and persons cannot be gainsaid. Either this was the perspective from the beginning of the nation or there

---

9. There are a number of theories put forward as to the actual facts of the case. One suggestion is that Genesis 2 (and 3) reflects more of the original "Oriental" myths, whereas Genesis 1 "reflects a careful distillation of everything mythological" in view of its longer and later development (chapter 1 is P, whereas 2 and 3 are J or JE). See, for instance, G. Von Rad, *Genesis: A Commentary*, 2nd ed., trans. J. Marks (Old Testament Library; London: SCM, 1966), 63, 72–73. See below for comments on this and other theories.

10. The most serious attempt to answer that question in recent times has been made by Mark Smith, in his several books. I will address those arguments in chapter 9.

must have been some cataclysmic experience that would have caused the systematic rewriting of all previous traditions. Outside of the exodus I see no such events.

To say that the exile was the event, as is increasingly common today, raises large issues. First of all, if the Israelites' thinking prior to the exile was characterized by continuity, then the destruction of their temple, their city, and their nation by the Babylonians should have been the death knell for their particular religion, as it was for the Ammonites, the Moabites, the Edomites, and the Philistines. Clearly in the world of cosmic reality, the gods of Babylon had utterly defeated Yahweh, and like Chemosh of Moab or Dagon of the Philistines, he should have been discarded. There is no reason for the Judeans to have concluded out of that event that their god was superior to the other gods, or even more shocking, that the other gods were not even real. They should have concluded the very opposite.

Second, one must either think that all the Old Testament literature was produced after the return from exile, or that it was completely rewritten in such a way as to leave intact all the accounts of Israel's worship of other gods against the backdrop of thoroughgoing transcendence. Either of these options seems to pose a historical impossibility. On the one hand, there is no way the Judeans could have emerged from the exile as they did, as "the people of the book," unless significant portions of the biblical literature had been in existence before the exile. So the biblical literature must have existed in some considerable form. It was not first written during and after the exile. By contrast, it is hard to imagine Dever's male elite (see note 20 in chapter 4 above) leaving intact the historical references to Israel's endemic apostasy if they were in fact rewriting the earlier documents to remove all traces of continuity thinking from them.

But leaving aside all these other issues (as well as increasing scholarly consensus that there was no exodus), suppose the exodus *was* the cataclysmic event. Could it not then be that the Genesis traditions were rewritten from the point of view of what was learned about God and reality out of those experiences? This is theoretically possible, but consider the implications. The Hebrews believed that God reveals himself through unique events and persons in time and space. This seems to be the reason their recording of that data is so much different from that of their neighbors.

What did they then think they were doing in rewriting the past to conform to their new understanding? (And this question must be raised if they were rewriting their past at any point in their history.) Had God not in fact acted in those previous times, but they were now making him appear to be doing so? Or was he acting then, but no one recognized it until now? This would mean that in this instance God was using a different mode of revelation than he used elsewhere in the Scriptures. Instead of inspiring the correct interpretation of his actions in time and space, he would have been giving interpretations for events whose historicity has been lost in tradition. These problems are not insuperable, but they do pose difficulties, especially for those who take the Bible's claim to have been revealed as the only satisfactory explanation for the book's characteristic ways of thinking.

Genesis

But leaving aside all those issues, what of the data itself in Genesis? Do the early chapters of Genesis give evidence of having once been myth in the phenomenological sense? It must be said that that evidence is very thin. As the chapters now stand, the key elements of myth are all conspicuously absent. There are no gods; there is no continual creation on the primeval plane that this world only reflects; there is no conflict between good and evil (or between order and chaos) on the metaphysical level as the precursor to creation; sexuality plays no part at all in creation; there is a high view of humanity, not a low one; and so on. If these chapters were once written in the parlance of myth, then they have been so thoroughly rewritten as to obliterate the earlier form.

Then why is it claimed that they do reflect a mythical outlook? It has been pointed out that in Genesis 1:1 the Hebrew permits the translation, "When God began to create the heaven and earth, the earth was without form and void." This is said to show that the Hebrews believed in preexistent chaos. For a response to this point, see chapter 4, above.

A second argument says that the order of creation is the same as that of the Babylonian creation myth. E. A. Speiser[11] puts it in this form:

---

11. E. A. Speiser, *Genesis* (Anchor Bible; Garden City, NY: Doubleday, 1964), 10.

Enuma Elish	Genesis
Divine spirit and cosmic matter are coexistent and coeternal	Divine spirit creates cosmic matter and exists independently of it
Primeval chaos; Tiamat enveloped in darkness	Earth a desolate waste, with darkness covering the deep
Light emanating from the gods	Light created
The creation of the firmament	The creation of the firmament
The creation of the dry land	The creation of the dry land
The creation of the luminaries	The creation of the luminaries
The creation of man	The creation of man
The gods rest and celebrate	God rests and sanctifies the seventh day

On the surface, the listing seems conclusive: the two understandings are identical. However, when one reads the two passages side by side, one will reach very different conclusions.[12] For one thing there are the proportions. In the *Enuma Elish* the first 160 lines are given over to an account of the emergence of the gods from chaos, their multiplication, the plan of the chaos monster Tiamat, and her consort Apsu, to kill the gods, and the war that results.[13] Where is this in Genesis? The second 130 lines have to do with the selection of Marduk as the champion of the gods. Where is this in Genesis? The next 138 lines discuss the reasons for Marduk's supremacy. Where is this in Genesis? The next 134 lines tell of the destruction of Tiamat. That is a total of 582 lines. Only then come five lines mentioning that Marduk hung up half of Tiamat's body to be the sky separating upper waters and lower waters. There follow 27 lines about the placement of the gods in the heavens.

---

12. The same thing is true in the case of many other supposed identical parallels. If one merely lists the characteristics of a human being and a dog, for instance (one nose, two eyes, two ears, hair, circulatory system, etc.), one will certainly conclude the two are essentially identical. However, if you actually put the two side by side, you will reach a very different conclusion.
13. See COS, 1:390 – 402 for the most recent translation.

The remaining 120 lines of this fifth tablet are broken. Speiser hypothesizes that the making of plants and animals on the earth was found here, but there is no evidence to support this position. What is clear is that the tablet ended with some request from the gods to Marduk, because tablet six begins with the statement that in response to that request Marduk made humans from mud and the blood of one of Tiamat's monsters in order to serve the gods and allow them to be at ease. There then follow 86 lines about building a heavenly sanctuary for Marduk, and finally 214 lines proclaiming the 50 names of Marduk.

To say, as Speiser does on the basis of this comparison, that "on the subject of creation biblical tradition aligned itself with the traditional tenets of Babylonian 'science' "[14] is not supportable from this evidence. There are a handful of superficial similarities, but in terms of the understanding of the nature of creation, the two are far apart. In fact, it is important to point out that the *Enuma Elish* is not about "creation" at all. The biblical term connotes the bringing into existence of something brand new, something that had not existed before. Thus, Genesis 1 is not about the emergence or emanation of the present world order from that which had always existed, namely, chaotic matter. Yet, this is what the Mesopotamian account, along with all other ancient Near Eastern "creation" stories apart from the Bible, is about.

Second, note that the *Enuma Elish* clearly has two purposes: to exalt Marduk and to promote the continuing victory of order over chaos. Genesis does not have either of those purposes. While it certainly does exalt Yahweh, that function is incidental to the main point, which is to say that the cosmos exists at the express will of the Creator and exists separately from him. Transcendence is everywhere understood. That is in direct contradiction to the Babylonian "science" of continuity.[15]

As to the supposed order of events, if Speiser's abstracted order is even to be considered a possibility, which a review of the total account renders unlikely, it is similar to that in Genesis only because both follow a broadly

---

14. Speiser, *Genesis*, 11.

15. Note that Gen. 1:21 explicitly says God "created" the great sea monsters. Not only are they not the basis of existence, but come far down in the account; they are the creation of God.

logical progression from general to specific, or lesser to greater. That hardly demonstrates a dependence of Genesis on the Mesopotamian account. If someone was starting with the kind of material and outlook found there, it strains credulity to imagine how he or she could possibly end up with Genesis 1:1 – 2:4. In particular is the function and place of humanity. What in the *Enuma Elish's* account of humans being made as an afterthought to allow the gods to be at ease could give rise to Genesis' having humans "created"[16] in the "image of God" to be given charge over all that God had created?

But none of what I have said must be construed to deny that there are similarities. For instance, there is the word for "deep" (Heb. *tehom*) in Genesis 1:2, which is etymologically related to the name of the Babylonian chaos monster, Tiamat. But what does this show? Only that Hebrew is a Semitic language like Akkadian. It is significant that *tehom* (which has a masculine form in Hebrew rather than the feminine form of Akkadian) is never used elsewhere in the Old Testament as a proper noun (Leviathan or Rahab being used instead), but is always used as a poetic expression for the inanimate seas, as it is used here ("darkness was upon the face of the *deep*, and the Spirit of God was hovering over the surface of the *waters*," lit. trans.). In this light I question whether the term was ever used of the chaos monster in Hebrew thought. To be sure, the word may have come to mean "deep" in the Semitic repertoire because of its original associations with Tiamat, but that does not mean the Hebrew writer would necessarily have had any awareness of that relationship. To the Hebrews, the Akkadian language of Mesopotamia was a barbarian, alien tongue (see Isa. 33:18 – 19).

Another similarity is the idea of something separating the upper waters (in the heavens) from the lower waters (on the earth and under the earth). But if the Hebrews may have shared the common ancient idea of the blue expanse above us being a hard surface that sometimes opens to let water fall

---

16. The word "create" (Heb. *bara'*) occurs five times in Genesis 1:1 – 2:4: 1:1, 21 (see previous note), 27; 2:3, 4. The first, fourth, and fifth occurrences are at the beginning and end of the account, framing it in such a way as to make it clear exactly what is being said. The second occurrence (the sea monsters) is possibly for polemic reasons, and that leaves the third (humanity), which must again be intentional. Humanity did not emerge as the highest of the beasts. Humanity is a distinctive creation of God. Note that the same point is made again in 5:1, 2, and 6:7.

on the earth, that is far from sharing the idea that that expanse is the body of a dead chaos monster and that the lights in it are the gods.

Beyond these details, what is striking is not what is similar in the biblical creation account to the other stories of origins found in Israel's world; rather, it is what is different. Thus Wolfram von Soden can write: "Direct influences of the Babylonian creation epic on the Biblical account of creation cannot be discerned."[17]

But if we leave Genesis 1:1 – 2:4 aside, what about all the frankly fantastic details in the 2:5 – 3:24: trees of life and knowledge, women from ribs, naming animals, talking snakes, and so forth? If they do not betray dependence on some known myth, surely those are the stuff of myth. This is where we need to think at our clearest, for this is where much of the discussion concerning myth is at its fuzziest. Myth, as I have tried to show in the previous chapters, presupposes much more than fantastic details. It is the reflection of a certain way of thinking about the world. To be sure, because of the way in which it thinks, the fantastic is often found in myth. But it is not the presence of the fantastic that makes a piece of literature myth; rather, it is the presence of the mythic worldview.

Once again, as in Genesis 1, Genesis 2 and 3 show a complete absence of the characteristic ideas of myth. There is a serious attempt to root the events in a specific place on earth. Whatever we make of the probable location of Eden, the writers are clearly saying that this is not some primeval place where the ideal reality exists continually.[18] They are saying that it was a distinct, particular place that could be located in this world. Furthermore, it is not continual divine action that determines the nature and condition of the human and natural world. Rather, shockingly, it is human decisions over profoundly ethical questions, taking place in time and space, that are responsible for the conditions now prevailing. There is no conflict between good and evil that brings creation into existence, nor is creation in any

---

17. W. von Soden, *The Ancient Orient: An Introduction to the Study of the Ancient Near East* (Grand Rapids: Eerdmans, 1994), 213. Gerhard Hasel went so far as to suggest that Genesis 1:1 – 2:4 was composed as a polemic *against* the Mesopotamian understanding of origins; see his "The Polemic Nature of the Genesis Cosmology," *The Evangelical Quarterly* 46 (1974): 81 – 102.

18. The land of "Dilmun" mentioned in the Myth of Enki and Ninhursag (see n. 3 in ch. 3) is clearly not intended to be understood as a definable place in our world of time and space.

sense the expression of divine sexuality. The serpent is in no way cosmic in nature, and his actions in no way determine the human responses. Neither is God threatened in any way by the serpent's attempt to subvert creation plans. In short, the whole catalogue of what I have described as the distinctive biblical understanding of reality is manifested here; none of the distinctive mythical ideas are present.

So how are we to explain the details? Surely if the present account had been rewritten from an original mythical formulation and these details had been endemic to that material, they would have been expunged in the rewriting process. That they have not been suggests strongly that no rewriting has taken place, but that both the absence of the mythical ground forms and the presence of these details were characteristic of the material from its inception. Those who hold such a position think of the story as poetic history. That is, it recounts genuine historic events, but does so in figurative and imaginative terms.

Perhaps the reason for doing this is to convey the meaning of events that, because of their distance from us both in time and substance, would be difficult to grasp in ordinary prose. Surely it must be said that if this was the purpose, the author has succeeded magnificently. The essential points are easy enough for a five-year-old to grasp, but the truths are profound enough that skilled scholars cannot plumb their depths. Be that as it may, whatever these chapters are, they are not myth. Similarities? Yes, there are, and we need not deny them or ignore them. But that is not the point. The point is the remarkable way in which the Bible assembles these components into a unique picture, one that is unlike anything before it or after it, apart from its derivations.[19]

The Psalms

On another front, we may look at such a psalm as Psalm 29, which has sometimes been called the Bible's "Canaanite psalm" because it can be paralleled from Ugaritic literature.

---

19. W. F. Albright, in his remarkable synthesis *Stone Age to Christianity*, 2nd ed. (Garden City, NY: Doubleday, 1957), points to the comparable example of Confucius. But while Confucius does root ethical behavior in the nature of things ("the Tao"), the impersonal nature of the Tao means that the motive for obedience is not relational. The Bible insists that beyond enlightened self-interest, we obey for love.

A psalm of David.
Ascribe to the LORD, you heavenly beings,
    ascribe to the LORD glory and strength.
Ascribe to the LORD the glory due his name;
    worship the LORD in the splendor of his holiness.
The voice of the LORD is over the waters;
    the God of glory thunders,
    the LORD thunders over the mighty waters.
The voice of the LORD is powerful;
    the voice of the LORD is majestic.
The voice of the LORD breaks the cedars;
    the LORD breaks in pieces the cedars of Lebanon.
He makes Lebanon leap like a calf,
    Sirion like a young wild ox.
The voice of the LORD strikes
    with flashes of lightning.
The voice of the LORD shakes the desert;
    the LORD shakes the Desert of Kadesh.
The voice of the LORD twists the oaks
    and strips the forests bare.
And in his temple all cry, "Glory!"
The LORD sits enthroned over the flood;
    the LORD is enthroned as King forever.
The LORD gives strength to his people;
    the LORD blesses his people with peace.

What is being said here? Obviously, Yahweh is being described in terms of the thunderstorm, and since Baal was the Canaanite storm god, it is often suggested that this psalm betrays the same understanding of Yahweh as the Canaanites had of Baal.[20] This point of view seems underlined when we note that just as Baal is called "the rider in the clouds," so on a few occasions Yahweh is said to ride in the clouds (see Deut. 33:26; Ps. 68:33; 104:3). But is that correct? Once again, we are dealing with superficial similarities and essential differences. We can notice that nowhere in the psalm is Yahweh

---

20. See, e.g., Mark Smith, *The Early History of God* (New York: Harper and Row, 1990).

identified with the thunderstorm. In fact, one can argue that the psalmist is at pains to avoid that implication. Just as Isaiah 40, in its antiidolatrous polemic, says that Yahweh sits above the circle of the earth, so here we are told that Yahweh sits above the flood. He is not the rain, nor is he the storm giving the rain. Can he be seen in them? Yes, but he is not to be identified with them. The pagan could say that Baal is not confined to the storm, but they could not say, given the law of continuity, that Baal is *not* the storm.

But what may well be going on here is something much like the contest on Mount Carmel, where Yahweh conclusively demonstrated that he, not Baal, was the One who gives rain. Thus here, whom does the thunder point us to? Baal? No! Anything that might be said of Baal in nature is much more the province of the one Creator of nature, Yahweh. Notice that the name Yahweh appears eighteen times in eleven bicola. The psalmist is making a point. So again, we have an example of a self-confident Yahwism appropriating language that would have been part of the repertoire of the day to say something that that language was not capable of saying on its own.

This point is seen even more clearly in Psalm 68, where in the context of his salvation of his people in history, God is said to be the rain giver (Ps. 68:8 – 9); moreover, the One who rides in the clouds is the One who rules all the kingdoms of the earth (vv. 32 – 35). In other words, the psalmist is saying that whatever might have been said of the gods could only truly be said of Yahweh. Psalm 104 makes much the same point. Yahweh is the sole Creator, the one who made Leviathan to play in the sea (!) (Ps. 104:26). The clouds are his chariot (v. 3), and the darkness is his handiwork. This is a hymn to the Transcendent One, and to suggest that because it contains allusions to the language of myth it is identical to myth is to misread it badly.

I want to say one further thing before I leave this discussion of the psalms. It is not surprising to find expressions in the Hebrew literature that have overtones of the typical expressions found in the world around Israel. It would be much more surprising to find no such points of contact. As the Bible insists, Israel was a fully participating part of its world. But in that light, notice how few these points of contact are. Where is any analogue in Ugaritic literature to the rest of the psalms? Where is any reflection on the *hesed* (unfailing love) or the endless faithfulness (truth) of Baal? Where else do laments end with the exultant vow of praise because of lamenter's complete confidence in his God?

The Ugaritic religious literature and the Israelite literature are like two circles that overlap to a slight degree at their respective edges. But the high point of the Ugaritic literature is the low point of the Israelite. Some may legitimately suggest that this shows that the Israelite point of view evolved from the Canaanite, and that will be addressed below. But what cannot be legitimately asserted is that the Ugaritic and the Israelite views are simply differing species of the same point of view. That, they definitely are not.

What I have attempted to do in this chapter is to show, not exhaustively, but I hope comprehensively, that the undoubted similarities to be found between the Bible and the religious literatures and practices of those cultures around Israel do not indicate a common way of thinking. I have argued that the writers of the Bible have consciously (and perhaps unconsciously, since they were a part of their world) utilized language, concepts, and even practices of the world around them to make the points they were trying to make. However, that they did so is not evidence that the Bible is really saying the same things that the world around was saying. I have argued that these similarities are not essential to what the Bible is saying. Rather, the Bible is using these things allusively, illustratively, and sometimes pejoratively to say something that is in fact radically different from the world around.

That they do so is no cause for us to modify our convictions concerning the Bible's uniqueness. To be sure, it is cause to clarify our claims concerning that uniqueness. It is not unique because it is not a part of its world; neither is it unique because its writers are incapable of relating what they say to that world. Rather, it is unique precisely because being a part of its world and using concepts and forms from its world, it can project a vision of reality diametrically opposite to the vision of that world.

PART 2

THE BIBLE AND HISTORY

CHAPTER 6

THE BIBLE AND HISTORY:
A PROBLEM OF DEFINITION

I observed above that one of the key distinctions, and perhaps the *key* distinction, between myth and the Bible is that whereas the myths are based in the interrelationships among the gods in primeval time and space, the Old Testament almost completely avoids such a basis.[1] Instead, the Old Testament depicts God's interactions with humans in the arena of unique, nonrepeatable events of time and space.[2] Clearly, in its conflicts with the alternative worldview and its claim to the exclusive validity of its understanding of reality, the Bible contends that these interactions actually occurred as they are depicted. The Jewish community and the church took this as a given up until the emerging domination of humanistic reason in the Enlightenment period. Because the intervention of God in the affairs of human beings cannot be made to conform to human reason, which is rooted in the uniform occurrences of all things in all times, the possibility of such divine-human interaction came to be ruled out a priori.

However, as I argued above, the very concept of history and of history writing is a result of the cross-fertilization of Greek and biblical thought. It can be cogently argued that Augustine's *The City of God* is the first expression of a philosophy of history to be found in the world. That human experience is moving toward a goal through a series of linked causes and effects in the visible world, that there is a linear progression to new causes

---

1. Job 1 – 2 and 1 Kings 22:19 – 23 are the only significant examples to the contrary; see the discussion in ch. 4.
2. This is not to argue that the Bible is a "history book" in the sense of a textbook, but rather, in the words of V. Philips Long, "that a historical impulse runs throughout the Bible, which, though not in every place and not always equally evident, is nonetheless pervasive" (*The Art of Biblical History* [Grand Rapids: Zondervan, 1994], 57).

and effects, with measurable progress toward a goal, and that there is real human choice and concomitant human responsibility — these ideas find their origin in the Bible and are brought to systematic expression with the aid of Greek thought. Thus, the idea that the Bible is not "historical" is something of an oxymoron.

DEFINITIONS OF HISTORY

But, as with "myth" a great deal depends on how we define the term *history*. What is history? Like the definition of myth, that of history is somewhat slippery. Nevertheless, there is a greater degree of consensus. The following would be representative:

> 1. an account of what has happened; narrative; 2. *a)* what has happened in the life of a people, country, etc.; *b)* a systematic account of this; 3. all recorded events of the past; 4. that branch of knowledge that deals systematically with the recording, analyzing, and coordinating of past events; 5. a known or recorded past: as, this coat has a *history*.[3]

As this definition makes clear, the term *history* functions at several levels. It may refer to the connected experience of something or someone in time and space. It may refer to the systematic record of such an experience. Or it may refer to a branch of knowledge. But we may say that this definition does not go deeply enough into the motive and method that go into a "historical" study of the past. The following definition by R. G. Collingwood deals with these issues more effectively: "History is a science (a systematic attempt to find out what is not already known) which seeks to discover actions of humans done in the past and to interpret that evidence for the purpose of human self-knowledge."[4]

This definition helps to focus the dictionary statement. History is *about human beings.* Technically, one cannot write a "history" of the solar system. Presumably it would be possible to write a narrative report of what one posits has taken place in the past in the solar system, but that is not a

---

3. *Webster's New World Dictionary of the American Language* (New York: World, 1970), 354 – 55.
4. R. G. Collingwood, *The Idea of History* (Oxford: Oxford Univ. Press, 1946), 9 – 10.

history, as Collingwood has framed it. Second, the reason for this systematic study is *for human self-knowledge*. A (necessarily) speculative account of the solar system's past will yield very little that will help us know ourselves better. A further point that emerges from reflection on Collingwood's statement is that the evidence will require interpretation that presupposes some standard of evaluation by which the significance of the data can be interpreted. Finally, "science" presupposes that the report of the evidence has not been falsified to suit the researcher's whims or presuppositions and that the correctness of the report is open to verification.

Let me attempt to summarize the above by offering another definition: *A history is a narrative of a series of events revolving about human beings acting in time and space. Existing for the purpose of human self-knowledge, it purports to be an accurate account of all significant elements in the series and includes an attempt to evaluate the relative importance of these elements for the eventual outcome.* Important components in this definition are the idea of connectedness among events, the centrality of human activity, the concept that significance is to be found in time and space, that accuracy in reporting is essential, that completeness is striven for, that evaluation is necessary, and that human self-knowledge is the end product.

UNDERSTANDINGS OF REALITY ON WHICH HISTORY WRITING DEPENDS

If one is to write history in the sense described above, certain ways of thinking about the nature of reality are prerequisite. If one does not understand reality in these ways, one will never embark on the historical enterprise. And if this understanding of reality is lost, history-writing will be lost with it. First, one must believe that humans are free and responsible. If we have no real choices to make, if all our choices are preconditioned by our past, by our relation to the invisible world of the gods, by our relation to the stars, by our fate, or even by our genes, there is no reason to ask what a person has chosen to do or why they chose to do it. We can learn nothing from their choices that will give us any wisdom about people and their choices or about our own choices and the relative merit of one choice over another. In fact, choice is an illusion.

Second, one must believe that causes and effects are linked and trace-able in time and space. If we believe that the primary causal connections are between the visible world and the invisible world, then there is no rea-son to attempt to understand what causes produce what effects, because all the causes are in the invisible world, which is beyond the reach of our research. The same will be true if we conclude that there is *no* necessary link between causes and effects (à la some existentialist thinkers). If we really do not know why anything happens in a world ruled by chance, then the recognition that something happened to someone in the past cannot possibly yield any information as to why that happened. This will also be the conclusion if we judge that all our actions are preconditioned by our ancestry and our past. Who could possibly know why a person did what they did? And since no other effect was possible, why bother to search for the causes?

Third, the researcher must believe that falsification of data is inimical to understanding. If he or she concludes that we can learn such and such from what certain persons chose to do in the past, and if it turns out that those persons did not exist and did not do those things, the conclusions are worthless. This is why Collingwood refers to history as a science. We trust the scientist's conclusions because we are confident he or she did not falsify the data being collected and studied. We may differ with the inter-pretation of the data, but the underlying assumption is that, whether the data agreed with the researcher's hypothesis or not, they were reported truthfully. All of this, of course, assumes the law of noncontradiction (see ch. 1), that something cannot be so and not-so at the same time, or, to put it another way, if two things are equal to a third thing, they are necessarily equal to each other. It also assumes that "true" facts are discoverable, that they exist.

Fourth, if one is to write history, he or she must believe that human experience is dynamic and goal-oriented. That is, it is possible for a human being to "transcend" his or her past and present and to accomplish some-thing that is not merely a repetition of the past or the present. If in fact we cannot change for the better (whatever we imagine that "better" to be), and if that change cannot really be for better or worse in light of what had been the case previously (movement toward a goal), then why study what people have done? Essentially there is nothing to be learned.[5] Thus the wry comment attributed to G. W. F. Hegel: "What experience and history teach is this — that people and governments have never learned anything from history."[6] On a more positive note is the comment attributed to George Santayana: "Those who can not remember the past are condemned to fulfill it."[7]

Fifth, relationships within time and space have fundamental significance. Two things are significant in that statement. The first is that what happens in this changing world is not to be passed over in the search for some unchanging "ideals." Rather, it is the study of these changes themselves that will yield "truth" — enduring understandings that will help to manage the changes and make the most of them. The second significant element in the statement is bound up in the word "relationships." If it is true that all things are not continuous with each other, it is also true that they are all connected with each other. That is, if persons, objects, ideas, and the like are indeed not identical with each other but are still dependent on each other, then it becomes important to know what each thing is in itself and how that "self" is then conditioned by its connections with other things that are not itself.

Sixth, there is some consistent standard by which behavior may be evaluated. That is, if you and I cannot agree, say, on what is the nature and destiny of humanity, then we will differ widely as to the meaning of any historical incident or incidents. I may say that the choices the persons made were effective and worthy of emulation, while you may say that the choices were foolish and blind. I may say they were bad choices and you may say they were good choices. A good case can be made that it was the agreement on what constituted virtues in Greek culture that allowed Thucydides and Herodotus to write the first Greek histories four hundred years before Christ, and we may also argue that it was the dissolution of this agreement that meant that with few exceptions, nothing comparable to Thucydides and Herodotus appeared

---

5. This seems to have been the point of view of the writer of the book of Ecclesiastes, who was apparently asking what can be learned from life apart from special revelation.

6. G. W. F. Hegel, *Philosophy of History* (New York: Collier, 1901), 5. Given his understanding of reality, this is perhaps not a surprising statement.

7. G. Santayana, *The Life of Reason* (New York: Collier, 1950), 253.

subsequently in Greece and Rome.[8] Ultimately, if there is no generally agreed-upon standard, the whole enterprise becomes bootless and will be abandoned, as appears to be happening in Western education today.

USES OF INFORMATION ABOUT THE PAST IN THE NONBIBLICAL ANCIENT NEAR EAST

Until recent times, the enterprise of history writing has been almost entirely a modern Western phenomenon. This is not to say that the ancients did not have an interest in "history," if by that we mean what happened in the past. They certainly did, but I would argue that their interest was not for the purpose of human self-knowledge or for progress toward the goal of human improvement. This becomes apparent when we see what kinds of information the ancients accumulated and how they used it. Information about the human past in the ancient Near Eastern literatures is of basically six sorts: omen texts, king lists, date formulae, epics, royal annals, and chronicles. In each of these cases, it is apparent that certain kinds of information from the past have been gathered and organized for some purpose considered worthwhile. However, that purpose is not accurate human self-knowledge.

Omens

Omen texts, if they do indeed have a historical basis, use historical data for nonhistorical purposes. An omen is a sign whose presence predicts the success or failure of a particular endeavor. Most frequently, these signs were found in four places: the entrails of a sacrificial animal, astronomical data, terrestrial data, such as patterns of bird flight and certain weather combinations, and dreams. The interpretations of the various conditions were contained in documents devoted solely to that subject. How much attention was given to this concern is indicated by the fact that the Babylonian omen texts run to some seventy volumes. Such an omen-text might read:

---

8. This Greco-Roman tradition of history writing tended to become more focused on rhetorical flourishes and political justification. The works of Livy (59 BC – AD 17) and Tacitus (56 – 120 AD) are somewhat of an exception to this norm in that they are concerned to use historical study as a way of combating what these two writers saw as a moral decline in Roman life.

If the liver is raised up and protrudes, the prince will go forth in power.

If the gall bladder is short, a foreigner will rule the throne.

If the teeth of the aborted animal protrude, the days of the king are at an end and another will sit upon the throne.[9]

The texts do not specify where these interpretations came from, but some scholars believe that they were derived from observation of the results when these same kinds of signs had appeared in the past.[10] Thus, given the principle of continuity, if the sign appears again, it is possible to predict that the same results will occur again. Obviously, there is no attempt to understand the effects and implications of human choices. Human choices have nothing to do with the outcome, and it is impossible to do anything to improve on that outcome. This material may indeed involve "history," but it is not history writing by any stretch of the imagination.

King Lists

King lists seem to constitute a kind of national genealogy in that the name and duration of the reign of each king is recorded. Here is an example from Sumer:

When kingship was lowered from heaven, kingship was first in Eridu. [In] Eridu A-lullim [became] king and ruled 28,800 years. Alalgar ruled 36,000 years. Two kings ruled it for 64,800 years.

I drop Eridu [because] its kingship was brought to Bad-tibira....

These are five cities, eight kings ruled over them for 241,000 years. The flood swept over. After the flood had swept over, when kingship was lowered from heaven, kingship was in Kish.[11]

Again, we may say that there could well be accurate information about the past here, at least in regard to the names and places. But this is not

---

9. On the omen texts, see A. L. Oppenheim, *Ancient Mesopotamia, Portrait of a Dead Civilization* (Chicago: Univ. of Chicago Press, 1964), 206ff.; see also COS, 1:423ff.

10. For an argument that omens should not be considered as historical, see P. Michalowski, "Commemoration, Writing, and Genre in Ancient Mesopotamia," in *Limits of Historiography: Genre and Narrative in Ancient Historical Texts*, ed. C. S. Kraus (Leiden: Brill, 1999), 69–90.

11. *ANET*, 265.

history writing as we have defined it above. There is no attempt at evaluation, and given the fantastic lengths of the individual reigns in some of the documents (e.g. 36,000 years for one king in the Sumerian list), we may doubt whether historical fact was a major concern. As noted above, the information was probably preserved as a kind of national genealogy.

Date Formulae

A third genre that illustrates the ancient Near Eastern use of information from the past is date formulae. Here each year of the reign of a king is given a title presumably based on some royal accomplishment during that year. Here are some examples from the reign of the Old Babylonian monarch Hammurapi:

1. Hammurapi [became] king
2. He established justice in the country
3. He constructed a throne for the main dais of the god Nanna in Babylon
4. The wall of [the sacred precinct] of Gagia was built
5. He constructed the *en.ka.as bar.ra*
6. He constructed the Sir of the goddess Laz
7. Uruk and Isin were conquered....
8. With the mighty power which Anu and Enlil had given him, he defeated all
9. his enemies as far as Subartu.[12]

As with the king lists, it seems likely that there is historical information contained in these formulae. But there is no analysis or evaluation and no basis for a better understanding of humanity or the human condition.

Epic

Another type of material relating to events in the past is the epic. Epics are typically narratives of certain events in the life of a hero, such as Gilgamesh in Sumerian literature or Ulysses in Greek literature. Many scholars now believe that these heroes and those of other national epics were historic individuals and that the legendary episodes told of them in the

---

12. *ANET*, 269–70.

epics had an original basis in fact. Presumably there was a Ulysses who fought at Troy and had a difficult time getting home. So also it seems likely there was a king of Uruk named Gilgamesh, who was something of an adventurer in early life but became more of a philosopher later on.

But to agree to these hypotheses is far from saying that the epics are historical in nature. In fact, the significance of the heroes is precisely that they have been lifted out of the narrow confines of specific history and made to be representative figures. The epics are in fact light philosophy in narrative form. They use some well-known figure from the past as a vehicle to present some rather profound reflections on the meaning of life. But they can only do this by taking from the hero the mundanely specific details of his life and then projecting him on the large screen of general humanity. He is only useful for the purpose of the epic if he is removed from the particularity of one proscribed human life and is elevated to the level of "Everyman."

Why do the epics make the hero a representative figure? They do this because of the principle of continuity. A specific individual is of little significance for general truth. The very things that make him or her specific are the things that are unimportant. It is insofar as that individual exhibits the characteristics of all humanity that he or she becomes significant. Thus, those who adhere to continuity have little interest in unique individuals and events. The very elements that are of interest to the history writer are of least interest to such persons.

Thus, Gilgamesh and Ulysses and the other heroes are deemed too important to be left in real time and space. They must be lifted out and made representative of all humanity in the timeless cycle of existence if the "truth" of their lives is to be known. But in a historical understanding, it is precisely the uniqueness of the individual that makes him or her significant. It is not participation in their life that is important. Rather, it is what may be learned from their particular experience that may be applied to our particular experience that is vital. Such an understanding cannot exist apart from a worldview of transcendence.[13]

---

13. Kenneth Kitchen observes that there are no examples in the ancient Near East of a movement in the other direction: historicizing of legend or myth (*On the Reliability of the Old Testament* [Grand Rapids: Eerdmans, 2003], 262). This is a significant point.

It is true that in the epics a much greater interest in human self-understanding is manifested than in the previous three genres. Given the conditioning to which continuity necessarily submits us, how shall we live? This is a question that thoughtful people address to their world. The answer is that we should live with courage, nobility, and shrewd wisdom. There are realities that we cannot change, but we can decide how those realities shall meet us.

In this regard it is interesting to compare Gilgamesh to Ulysses, and then Ulysses to the Greek dramas. It is possible to see an interesting refinement in the character development, in the plot line, and in the way the questions are addressed. Nevertheless, the Greek dramas are not historical. However much we may admire Antigone's courage and nobility and however much we may sympathize with her in her dilemma, there is no question of her being a historical personage or of the drama recounting her actual life and decisions.

Royal Annals

In the fifth type of material, the royal annals, we find much better examples of a thoroughgoing kind of collection and recording of data from the past. Those from Assyria in the first millennium BC are best known, but there are excellent specimens from several other ancient Near Eastern nations as well. These annals record in considerable detail many of the events in each reign. Sweeping military victories and the completion of vast building projects are favorite topics. Interestingly, defeats and failures are never reported. In every event the king is central, whether as strategist or as tactician. The annals were typically inscribed on the walls of the temple of the major deity of the kingdom. Here is an example from the annals of Sargon, an Assyrian king from 721 – 705 BC:

> I besieged and conquered Samaria, and led away as booty 27,290 inhabitants of it. I formed from among them a contingent of 50 chariots and made the remaining inhabitants assume their positions. I installed over them an officer of mine and imposed upon them the tribute of the former king. Hanno, king of Gaza, and also Sib'e the vizier of Egypt set out from Rapihu against me to deliver a decisive battle. I defeated them;

Sib'e ran away, afraid when he heard the noise of my army, and has not been seen again. Hanno, I captured personally.[14]

These royal annals have been of great value in reconstructing the history of the ancient Near East. For instance, they list with great care the names of all defeated nations along with their kings and officials. This has been helpful in working out the political topography of the region in various periods as well as making it possible to reconstruct the chronology of that first millennium BC. Of course the annals are most useful when we have parallel records from two opposing nations and the two can be balanced against each other. For instance, when both claim to have visited a resounding defeat on the other in a particular battle, the likelihood of a draw begins to suggest itself as the actual fact.[15]

But in spite of the significant amounts of historical material the royal annals contain, they cannot be considered to be history. The chief reason is their purpose. They exist to glorify a king, not to promote more accurate understanding of the world in general and of humanity in particular. Thus they are accurate and complete only insofar as what is reported reflects favorably on the king. By the same token, there is no attempt to evaluate behaviors in order to discover which were successful and which were not. From the annalist's perspective, everything the king did was successful. Furthermore, there is no standard beyond the achievement of that king's particular goals by which to make a judgment as to success or failure. For these reasons, the annals can be considered to contain historical data but not to be actually historical.

The purpose of glorifying the king is certainly one of the reasons why the annals do not report defeats and failures. But another reason such events are not reported is related to the principle of continuity. To record failures and defeats is to run the real risk of causing them to be repeated. If reports of the kinds of things the king does not want to happen again are suppressed and reports of things he would like to see happen again are recorded in some detail, the risks are minimized.

---

14. *ANET,* 284 – 85.

15. See, for example, the Egyptian and Hittite annals of the battle of Qadesh in 1297 BC (*ANET,* 256 – 57, 319).

Chronicles

The genre of ancient Near Eastern literature that most nearly accords with what we think of as history writing is the chronicle, found primarily in the so-called Babylonian Chronicle Series.[16] In its complete form this series encompassed the history of Babylon from the beginnings of the neo-Babylonian period (747 BC) until the middle of the Seleucid period (226 BC). Unfortunately, it is not complete. Unlike the annals, which had a heavily propagandistic motive, the Babylonian chronicles exhibit a much more objective tone, recording defeats as well as victories. The focus is largely on the kings and their succession; as Sparks says, "they seem to exhibit a genuine intellectual interest in the history of Babylon itself."[17] But even here, the purpose behind the recording is not clear. Sparks suggests that it is another example of the penchant for lists among the Mesopotamians.[18] Here it is a list of kings and their accomplishments, but without any real attempt to evaluate the significance of these accomplishments. Again, we are left with a collection of historical data, but not a history.

REASONS FOR THE ABSENCE OF HISTORY WRITING

Focus on "Now"

If we agree that there is no history writing per se in the ancient Near East (or in the Far East, for that matter), we may ask why. The answer, I believe, lies in the worldview of continuity. In the cycle of existence, all that matters is "now" and its continuation in the most comfortable, pleasurable, and secure manner possible. Since all things recur endlessly, there is no future different from the present, and there is no past from which the present differs. In such a circumstance, study of the past for the sake of improvement of the present and the future makes no sense. One can only hope to discover a pattern of recurrences in the past that will either illuminate similar recurrences in the present or perhaps facilitate the recurrence

---

16. COS, 1:137, 467–68.
17. K. Sparks, *Ancient Texts for the Study of the Hebrew Bible* (Peabody, MA: Hendrickson, 2005), 369.
18. Ibid., 370–71.

of positive patterns. The idea that the past could be in any way transcended would be not only nonsensical, but even more, subversive.

Subjective Orientation

The worldview of continuity also dictates what we may call a "subjective" orientation. As we have seen, history writing calls for an "outside" perspective on persons and events, the possibility of abstracting oneself in some sense, even if limited, from what one is describing in order to allow the data to say whatever they will. But in continuity, there is no "outside." What matters is not discovery, but maintenance. Reality is about me and mine, so whatever works to promote my, our, goals, desires, and continued existence is necessarily good.

This explains the personalization of the forces of the cosmos. All objects are viewed personally. In fact, there are no objects — thus, there is no "object" of thought; nothing is considered for itself apart from its impact on me. Ultimately, it only has existence as it relates to me. The idea that my, our, good could be promoted by something outside of myself, ourselves, is utterly foreign to the worldview of continuity. Ultimately, the only valid response is, "How do I feel about this?"

Multiplicity of Causes

Furthermore, in the worldview of continuity there is an almost unlimited multiplicity of causes. If ultimate reality is a mirror image of proximate reality, then reality is irredeemably multiple. Looking at the world around us in that light, we can see that any attempt to understand why anything happens is foolish. There are literally thousands of divine forces at work in the world, all shaping what we do in a myriad of ways. The idea that human choices in the past have any influence on what is happening in the "now" simply does not rate consideration. It is infinitely more likely that it is the position of the stars that explains what is happening in the "now."

Determinism

This latter point brings up another factor growing out of continuity. This is determinism. Given the cyclical and interconnected nature of reality, choice is merely an illusion. We really have no choices to make. Everything we "choose" to do is dictated by forces outside of ourselves. Just as a cog in a machine has no choice in how it participates in the action of the machine, so a person will do what their place in the machine of the cosmos dictates, whether they are aware of it or not. To be sure, if one can understand the motion of the machine and how it impinges on one, then it might be at least possible to cooperate freely and minimize friction. Thus, we have the part played by the horoscope: you can fight your fate and be crushed, or you can cooperate with it and be more comfortable.

I vividly recall overhearing a young woman telling another young woman about her divorce. She said, "We should have known better than to get married; everybody knows a Leo and a Capricorn can't live together." Obviously, if there is no genuine choice; there is no responsibility, which is generally comforting. But neither is there any point in studying those actions with a view to understanding how they affect the outcome. The outcome is predetermined.

Preoccupation with Order and Security

There is also in the worldview of continuity a preoccupation with order and security. That is because it is clear on the principle of analogy that the cosmos is a battleground between opposing forces: the forces of construction versus the forces of destruction. Chaos is always hovering about us, whether physically, materially, or politically. The ultimate goals of comfort, pleasure, and security are completely dependent on the continual victory of order. On the surface, at least, time spent in a study of human actions in the past, particularly unique, nonrepeated ones, seems to have no pay-off in assisting the victory of order. Rather, it seems likely that intensive study of the recurring patterns of nature, society, and the human psyche would yield much more information about how to get oneself in line with those recurrences in such a way as to experience a maximum of order.

THE BIBLE'S UNIQUE APPROACH TO HUMAN-HISTORICAL EXPERIENCE

Humans Treated as Real Individuals

When compared with the examples above, the Bible exhibits profound differences. If it is agreed that there are significant differences between the Bible and modern history, the differences between the Bible and the ancient "historical" materials are still more significant. Note that the biblical characters are not depicted as semidivine, representative beings. They are clearly presented to us as unique individuals, firmly rooted in time and space. Abraham is no Gilgamesh, nor are his adventures those of Everyman. Even a Samson, whose exploits often seem to have a legendary flavor about them, is clearly presented to us as a historic individual who lived in a specific place and time. This emphasis on the individual is of great importance because it is in such contrast to the rest of the ancient world. The Bible insists that truth is not to be found in the norms but in each one whose individuality transcends the norms.

Failures and Defeats Not Glossed Over

Furthermore, the Bible is remarkably frank about its heroes' failures and defeats. Consider Abraham, the man of faith, lying about Sarah when he gets into a difficult spot, or David, the man after God's own heart, casually ordering the death of a faithful soldier so that he, the king, can cover his own sin with the soldier's wife. Then there is Solomon, the wisest man on earth, who is foolish enough to enter into a myriad of marriage covenants with pagan wives, necessarily diverting him from covenant loyalty to Yahweh.

It does not matter that these are all heroes of their respective narratives. Clearly, there are standards outside of the character's own wishes and goals by which he may be judged. But by the same token, the accounts do not glory in the failures of the heroes, as is the case in the Greek heroic literature. The failures are simply tragic, with no trace of the heroic about them. So the reports not only reveal a concern for integrity of reporting, but also a capacity for evaluation of behavior. Success or failure is no longer determined by the apparent and the immediate.

Significance of Relationships

Beyond this, the Bible evinces a serious attempt to portray the significance of relationships among events and persons. The portion of 2 Samuel and 1 Kings that begins at the sin with Bathsheba and ends with Bathsheba's son Solomon on the throne is surely one of the great examples of all time in this thoughtful exploration of interrelationships. We see David's inability to deal forthrightly with his children's sins, but yet his continuing political acumen. We see the tragedy of Amnon and Tamar and the power of lust. We see the growing alienation of Absalom.

In all of this, there are no simplistic solutions or easy attributions of causes. Many factors enter in, and the text seems to treat all of them with the same straight-forward neutrality. It is also important to note, in the light of the discussion of divine intervention below, that there is no *deus ex machina* in these accounts. Clearly what David and Solomon chose to do was done, and judged, in the light of the truth of the transcendent Yahweh, but he exercised no cosmic control over the choices.

Significance of Human Choices

Thus the Bible demonstrates a conviction that it is human choices that shape the direction of events on earth. The narrative we were just describing is one classic example, but there are many others. The persons may well be responding to some divine initiative, but yet they have real choices to make and the results reflect their choices, not some fated correspondence to a divine drama. This is not to say that divine providence is not seen working through, and sometimes in spite of, these choices, but it is to say that events are never predetermined apart from the human factor. This is a real world and these are real choices.

Developmental Relationships

The Bible also exhibits a sense of movement from one point to another in its recounting of events. There is nothing of this sort in the rest of the ancient world, even in its best effort, the royal annals. The relation of one reign to the next, whether it was better or worse than the last, or how its accomplishments compared to reigns of similar circumstances, is clearly of no concern to the annalists. Only repetitious reports of ever-recurring successes in the here and now occupy their attention.

Against this backdrop we see the Bible comparing David to Saul, or noting that Jeroboam set the stage for two hundred years of royal godlessness in Israel, or reporting that Josiah was a better king than any since Hezekiah. Against a view of time that is clearly cyclical, with events on the cycle being related not to each other but to the cyclical pattern itself, we see an understanding that is predominantly linear with the upward or downward direction of that line being determined by the impact of the combination of events in relation to each other.[19]

Implications of Transcendence for Israel's View of Human-Historical Experience

Laying aside for the moment whether these characteristics qualify the Bible to be called historical or not, we must ask where they come from. They are dramatically different from the approach to the past found all around Israel. Once again, the answer is transcendence. The recognition that God is not a part of this psycho-socio-physical world gives rise to all the other differences. As we have already noted, monotheism, creation, purpose, the importance of personality, ethics, and the significance of uniqueness all flow from the concept of transcendence. But in addition to these, transcendence makes it impossible to believe that human events are merely corresponding to their opposite numbers in the divine realm. There is no essential connection between the two. The connection is interpersonal and relational.

Possibility of Transcending Events

One of the implications of transcendence is that it is now possible to get outside of the events themselves. There is a realm beyond the cosmos, and this makes a space, as it were, for looking at persons and events from a perspective beyond mere self-interest. When this is coupled with the idea of purposive creation, there enters the picture an outside perspective from which to judge all things. Famously, in Joshua, Judges, Samuel, and Kings, this is the perspective of the covenant, as that covenant was presented in the book of Deuteronomy.

Today it is fashionable to refer to "the Deuteronomic Historian." Whether there was such a person, or whether the court prophets (Nathan,

---

19. R. A. Oden ("Myth and Mythology [OT]," *Anchor Bible Dictionary*, ed. D. N. Freedman [Garden City, NY: Doubleday, 1995], 4:948), says that the idea of linearity in Israel's thought is a "cliché." But what else are we to see in the collection from Genesis to Kings but a line from creation to the exile?

Iddo, and Gad, who are the ones the Bible identifies as being responsible for the materials) simply all shared a devotion to the Mosaic covenant, is not critical to this discussion. What is significant is that it was the underlying concept of transcendence that made possible such a stunning departure from anything similar in the world around. There is a single outside perspective from which to judge and interpret the events of an entire millennium. Since the Transcendent is necessarily one, it begins to become possible to find a single thread running through apparently diverse events.

Impossibility of Misleading God

Furthermore, transcendence means that God cannot be duped. If the gods are part of the system, then it is possible to manipulate the system and manipulate the gods. Thus, if we record the past *as it should have been* (given present needs) often enough and loud enough, that is indeed what the past was. The past, like everything else, only exists to serve the present; it has no existence of its own. But the transcendent God cannot be manipulated. He exists outside of time and space, and he knows what actually took place. There is no point in denying the sins of David; they cannot be erased by denial.[20]

Of course, an additional element is that this particular transcendent One is absolutely reliable — he is true. It is remotely conceivable that the Transcendent could be a liar, although it is difficult to conceive of a universe where nothing could be relied on. But in any case, it does not pertain to this universe. Here, the One who stands beyond and behind all things, encompassing them with himself, does not lie and does not permit his followers to do so. Thus, the idea of recording events of the past in ways that do not accord with the facts in order to manipulate reality becomes an exercise in futility.

All of this helps us to understand a feature of Israelite life that is otherwise inexplicable. That feature is the so-called "prophetic immunity."

---

20. In this regard, it is significant that the Hebrew word *dabar*, normally translated "word," also has the connotations of "event" and "thing." Words have an existence, a reality, of their own, and that reality cannot be altered at will.

Among Israel's neighbors, it was common for the kings to maintain a "stable" of professional prophets. We know of one Israelite king, Ahab, who did the same, and there may well have been others. As noted above, these persons were on a salary and existed to enable the king to divine the future. Obviously, it was in their best interests to stay in the king's good graces. If they should have something negative to say, they had better say it in the most palatable way possible.

But these are not the persons responsible for that section of the Hebrew Bible called "The Prophets." The persons responsible for these books and what is said in them were not maintained by the kings or the wealthy, and what they had to say was notably *very* negative toward all those interests. Yet they continued to speak out with impunity, and if kings often contrived to find ways to kill them, they were hardly ever able to do so outright. Why? Because those men and women spoke for the transcendent God, who stood outside of time and space. They were not there to make the king successful; they were there to hold him accountable to a divine standard that no king could change.

Thus, a Nathan, face to face with a king furious over an injustice done in his kingdom, could look that king in the eye and say, "You are that man," and a good deal more, and walk out of the throne room alive (2 Sam. 12:1 – 12). Likewise, the most that a cynical Jehoiakim could do to a Jeremiah who was denouncing everything Jehoiakim stood for was burn Jeremiah's scroll in a brazier (see Jer. 26:1 – 19; 36:1 – 32). In the light of this commitment to a truth about things that stood outside of the superficial well-being of the moment, the Bible's identification of the prophets as the historians of Israel makes perfect sense.

A Simplified Understanding of Causation

Furthermore, transcendence offers a simplified understanding of causation. For many, one of the more troublesome aspects of Old Testament teaching is its forthright assertions that Yahweh is the one who brings about evil (see Isa. 44:7; Amos 3:6). To be sure, we must think our way through the implications of such statements carefully, but much more important than their troublesome nature is the breath-taking uniqueness of these statements, which should capture our attention.

Everywhere else in the world, the presence of evil has been explained with dualism. That is, there are two eternal entities: positive (from the human point of view because it is favorable to our continued existence) and negative (because it is unfavorable).[21] In the Bible alone that way of thinking is expressly denied. It is the one God who is responsible for all that is.[22] There is nothing beyond him and there is nothing besides him; he has no rival on any level.[23]

What this means is that all that happens is either in defiance of, or in compliance with, Yahweh's creative purposes. He is the first cause, and everything can be understood in terms of a limited number of causes flowing from that first cause. How different this is from that which emerges from

---

21. This is not to suggest that one of these is ontologically "better" than the other, any more than the positive pole of a battery is better than the negative one. In fact, they are both essential to the cosmos as we know it. Thus, we consider death to be an evil, and it is for us personally; but actually death and decay are essential to the continuation of life on the planet, and our personal existence only has meaning as one small expression of the continual life principle. This is why the continuity worldview places little value on individual life and why it is basically apathetic toward "evil."

22. It is almost ludicrous to attempt a brief treatment of such a complex subject, but for the reader's sake, I cannot avoid trying to point out at least the key issues in the discussion. As Genesis 1 – 3 show, "good" in the Bible is that which accords with the Creator's purposes in creating, and "evil" is that which does not conform to that purpose. This in itself is an astonishing innovation. Thus, "the knowledge of good and evil" of Genesis 2 – 3 is the ability to define the purpose of one's existence for oneself. Truly that is to be "like God," and the desire for such is at the heart of human sinfulness. It is important, then, to recognize that the Hebrew word ra‘ connotes much more than does the English word "evil." It encompasses everything from "misfortune" to "perversion" and everything in between — anything that is contrary to God's plan for the world. Now, does God *make* people choose to do what is contrary to his plan? Is that what it means for God to "cause" evil? While there are some who would insist that is the case, I would argue that there is good biblical evidence against that opinion. Rather, what is meant is *if the possibility of rejecting the good exists, it is because God has responsibly chosen to allow that possibility to exist.* That is, God is the first cause, though not the effective cause.

23. The incipient dualism of a good deal of popular Christian teaching is a witness to the power of this way of thinking. In such teaching Satan assumes the role of the negative entity, while Jesus takes on the role of the positive entity, and the world is the shadowy battleground reflecting their ongoing struggle in the real, heavenly realm. We, the "pawns on the board," as it were, must do our best to enable Jesus to continually defeat Satan. Any Egyptian or Babylonian would have felt perfectly at home with such a view of things.

the perspective of the closed cosmos of continuity, where there are an almost infinite number of causes for anything that happens. In such a perspective any attempt to define *the* cause of an action is almost always futile.

As noted in an earlier chapter, Henri Frankfort, using a sociological/theological definition of myth, said that Israel had replaced the myth of recurring cycles of nature with the myth of the will of God.[24] While I think his use of the term myth is inaccurate, his basic observation is correct. The central concept of Israel's religion is that the transcendent Yahweh has a revealed will for human life and that all activity can be evaluated in the light of that will. Furthermore, his divine purpose to bless all humanity through the revelation of himself is the thread that unites all of Israel's experiences, whether they are in line with that purpose or in defiance of it.

But at this point it may be objected that the simplification of causality just discussed could easily lead to a determinism that would be just as rigid as the fates in the system of continuity. Things would happen solely because God determined them, and any attempt to understand the human element in them would be bootless at best. That could certainly be the case in the Old Testament, but it is not. The reason it is not the case is because of the personality of the First Cause. Unlike the gods, who are impersonal forces given human-like faces to render them more understandable and controllable, Yahweh is a full-orbed person.[25]

It is precisely the complexity of Yahweh's personhood that has troubled many theologians who would like to have a God who is immutable and impassible. His affections and his rages, his shrewdness and his compassion, his tenderness and his implacability, all against the backdrop of unfailing *hesed* and absolute trustworthiness, have proven a treasure-trove for reflection and meditation across the centuries. Since humans are also personal, and yet discontinuous with God, this has meant that personal relationships, both between human and God and human and human,

---

24. H. Frankfort, *Before Philosophy* (London: Penguin, 1949), 244.

25. The history of the word "person" is most interesting. Originally Lat. *persona* did in fact refer to the masks that actors wore. But then during the Trinitarian debates, the term began to be used to describe Father, Son, and Holy Spirit within the unity of the Godhead: "one God in three *persons*." Thus, the modern understanding of personhood and what it involves got its impetus from the "personal" characteristics of the God of the Bible.

become significant. It is clear that while God does indeed want obedience, something he could determine at will, he is much more interested in loving relationships, something that cannot be determined. Thus, simplified causation does *not* result in determinism, and the study of relationships becomes profoundly significant.

Speech as the Mode of Accomplishing Divine Purposes

This understanding of the personal nature of the transcendent One has another implication for our study. That has to do with the mode of revelation. How is One who is at the same time transcendent and personal to accomplish his purposes with persons in the world? Clearly he could not do so through mechanical manipulation. This would be to violate the very nature of personal interaction. Neither could he do so through recurring and repetitive cycles. This would be to devalue individual persons and the significance of their constantly changing and developing personal landscapes. What he chose to do, according to the Bible, was to enter into their lives through the medium of speech in the context of their ongoing experiences, that is, their personal, and then national, history.

Here we come to the mystery of language. How is it that persons who are radically discontinuous with each other, as we are, are able to enter into one another's lives and build meaningful webs of relationship? It is through constantly changing and developing dialogue. It is through language that we can transcend ourselves and reach out and into the life-experience of another.[26]

In other words, relationships can be searched for and found. Moreover, since we are discontinuous with God, we cannot participate in his life or receive his blessings through magical means. Any attempt to do so is met in the Bible with the bitterest of denunciations.[27] Magic is a denial both of

---

26. Recently, a noted psychologist who has studied monkeys for some time has said that the capacity for language (not merely ability to communicate) separates humans from the other primates so completely that the mode of cognition of a chimpanzee is probably closer to that of a beetle than it is to that of a human (J. Adler, "Thinking Like a Monkey," *Smithsonian* [January 2008], 62).

27. Interestingly, magic is not denounced, as in the nineteenth- and early twentieth-century West, because it does not work. Whether it works or not, and often enough it does, is beside the point. The Bible denounces it because it is *ra*ᶜ — an attempt to use the world in ways it was never intended to be used.

transcendence and of personhood, an attempt to mechanically manipulate another for one's own benefit while bypassing any meaningful relationship with that other.

So how *do* we participate in the life of God and receive his blessings? We do so by emulating his ethical character, that is, by being holy as he is holy. And we do that in ongoing and developing relationships with him and with other humans. Since we humans cannot ascend to heaven through correspondence or continuity, God has had to reveal himself and his purposes in the arena of time and space on earth. But the primary mode of revelation is not in the recurring events of nature; it is in the unique events of human-historical experience, those that transcend the normal and continuous.

No longer is the actual downgraded in order to discover the Ideal, for the Ideal has come to clothe himself in the actual. Thus it becomes incredibly important to know what actually happened, what the Ideal actually said, and how the human partners actually responded. It is especially in human activity, and more especially, in human activity involving ethical choice, that revelation can occur. Moreover, the rightness or wrongness of those choices can be evaluated in the light of the single divine purpose. All of this provides the motive for recording history.

HISTORY WRITING AS MYTH-MAKING?

But could we not say that the Old Testament has simply replaced the nature myth of Israel's neighbors (and some would say, of early Israel herself) with a history myth?[28] I take this to mean that Israel has simply chosen another vehicle to express her faith. Whereas Israel's pagan neighbors used the vehicle of nature, Israel used the vehicle of history. Different, yes. Unique, no. Both cultures are doing essentially the same thing, using some aspect of the present world to express an otherworldly perspective.

While this suggestion sounds plausible on the surface, it suffers from a serious flaw. That flaw is that the two cultures are not doing the same thing with their "vehicle." For the pagans, nature *is* the gods. To be sure, as I have

---

28. W. T. Stevenson, *History as Myth: The Import for Contemporary Theology* (New York: Seabury, 1969).

said above, this is not to say that the gods were thought to be limited to nature, but they and the natural forces were continuous with each other. Nature was not merely the stage on which the gods appeared, it was not merely the vehicle for faith; rather, the stage and the actors were identical. For Israel (unlike some modern thinkers, on which see the discussion in ch. 8), there was no identification of Yahweh with the history in which he appeared. Again, this is due to the thoroughgoing way in which transcendence permeates biblical thinking. Nothing in this cosmos — neither events, persons, forces, nor processes — was to be identified with Yahweh. He transcended them all.

Probably the Hebrews' lack of philosophical sophistication stood them in good stead on this point. Clearly, abstractions did not interest them much. When they wished to say that something was made of wood, they simply pluralized the noun "wood," making it "woods." Likewise, they did not care to distinguish between cognitive and volitional. The person who had disobeyed God had "forgotten" him, and "to hear someone's voice" was to obey that person. A century and a half ago it might have been said that the Hebrews were incapable of thinking in abstractions. No one who is acquainted with ancient, or so-called "primitive," cultures would say that today. To *choose* to think in certain ways and to *be able* to think in certain ways are two different things. So the Hebrews, being generally impatient with abstractions, were much less likely to create an abstraction such as "history" and then hypostatize it. Leave that to nineteenth-century European philosophers like Hegel.

But beyond their manner of thinking, the Bible betrays another important factor that separates its approach to "vehicles of faith" from that of Israel's neighbors. Whereas it is clear that these neighbors looked long and deeply at the world as it is and arrived at an understanding of the world in which its recurring processes are divine, that is not what Israel did on the testimony of the Bible. Had Israel for some reason looked at their personal and historical experiences and used those to create a faith, it is at least arguable that they might have deified the historical processes. But, according to their testimony, that is exactly what did not happen. Instead, this transcendent God kept breaking into their experience and smashing their easy interpretations, twisting them out of all recognizable shape. For according to their testimony, whenever *they* created a theology based on their history, they got it wrong. One classic example goes like this:

1. Our existence as a people in this land, against all the odds, proves God has chosen us.
2. David's choice of Jerusalem was clearly inspired by God.
3. The glorious temple of Solomon, incomparable in the world, is clearly home to the supreme God.
4. The God of David's dynasty, God of Jerusalem's temple, has promised to bless us.
5. God's promises cannot fail.
6. *Therefore*, our historical choices are infallible and we cannot be defeated.

Like their pagan neighbors, the Israelites were constantly trying to fit the divine into a box of their own making so that the divine could be understood and controlled. Clearly, they forgot what their own doctrine of creation told them: God is the infinite Creator, who cannot be boxed in. Unlike the gods, who *are* the recurring system and thus are incapable of doing anything new, Yahweh is outside this system, its Maker, and he rejoices to do things that have never happened before. Will he be consistent? Absolutely! Will he be predictable on our terms? Never!

Thus, the prophets, whose importance cannot be overstated, were continually declaring on God's behalf, "I am not the prisoner of your experience. If I will not allow you to idolize the thunderstorm, neither will I allow you to idolize your interpretation of your life experiences." So Yahweh was constantly standing over against what they were doing: judging it, remaking it, reinterpreting it.

It is often said, "The winners write history." But that is exactly what Yahweh would not allow to happen. He told them what their history meant, and it was usually quite different from what the rich and the powerful would like to have had said about it and about themselves. In the end, the idea that the God of these little Canaanite principalities called Israel and Judah was in fact using the mightiest powers of the world to discipline and refine his people was the last thing that anyone would have expected to emerge from Israel's historical experience. For in the end, Israel's history is tragedy compounded by tragedy.

Here is what the Israelites could have thought:

+ We were really arrogant to think that ours was the only God; now we know better.
+ We were much too exclusive in our thinking, believing that there is only one way to express one's faith; now we know better.
+ Our spare and limited expressions of faith could be enriched by the rich religious pageantry and imagery of our captors.
+ Our reliance on a book religion — verbal communications from God about the way we conduct our lives — needs to be replaced with the much more satisfying ritual participation in the great cosmic dance.

But what was the actual meaning of that experience as testified through the prophets? It was the very opposite of the reasonable conclusions above. The exile was intended to teach the Judeans that Babylon's gods were not gods at all; Judah's problem was that they had not been monotheistic enough.

+ The exile was intended to teach the Judeans that covenantal obedience is indeed the only way to express faith; Judah's problem was that they had not been exclusivist enough.
+ The exile was intended to teach the Judeans that ritual is only symbolic of genuine changes in personal relations between the worshiper and God; Judah's problem was that they had been too much infected with the ritualistic understandings inherent in the worldview of continuity.
+ The exile was intended to teach the Judeans that it is by means of the Word of God that we will be delivered from entrapment in the cosmic plunge; Judah's problem was that they were already too much entrapped in attempts to control the cosmos for their own benefit.

All this is to say that according to the testimony of the Bible, whenever Israel tried to entangle God in the box of their interpretation of history, he kept breaking out of the box, forcing them to hear another understanding of that history that was largely alien to what they wanted to hear. The prophets continually call them to look through and then beyond their experiences, surrendering their lust for control, releasing themselves in radical trust of a God who though he appeared in their history was as far beyond it as he was beyond the thunderstorm. Thus, to say that Israel's approach to reality was identical to that of their neighbors with the unimportant difference that Israel expressed its faith through "history-myth" while its neighbors expressed theirs through "nature-myth" is both to use "myth" in an impermissibly broad way and to fail to understand the impact of transcendence on the whole approach to "vehicles for faith."

Thus, the Hebrew does not bear witness to his faith by a reenactment of great cosmic or natural dramas for control purposes. Neither does he bear witness to his faith by retelling a fictional recreation of the past for control purposes. Rather, he recites the ways in which God has intervened in the experience of the Israelites, both as individuals and as a nation, as interpreted by God through his own prophets. The upshot of the recitation, when constrained by the implications of transcendence, is history writing.

CHAPTER 7

IS THE BIBLE TRULY HISTORICAL?
THE PROBLEM OF HISTORY (I)

I n the previous chapter I discussed the nature of historiography and tried to show how the biblical worldview provides the basis for genuine history writing. Nevertheless, when the biblical accounts are compared with modern history writing as per the above definition, it is plain that the Bible differs in many respects. For instance, the accounts are by no means exhaustive, often leaving large gaps; divine causation is frequently referred to; the standard by which progress or lack of progress in events is judged is the outworking of the divine purpose; and the style is more anecdotal than analytical.

Thus, it has become customary in some circles to refer to the Bible as being "history-like"[1] or as containing "historical fiction."[2] Thus, we must address two questions: Is it fair to call the biblical accounts "history," and does it matter in the end whether these accounts are historical or not? I will take up the first question in this chapter and the second in the following one.

In answering the first question, we must address at the outset the issue of divine purpose, causation, and intervention. Typically today historians will argue that "history" assumes complete human responsibility for events and their outcomes; thus, to the extent that divine involvement enters the discussion the material is unhistorical.[3] Interestingly, Collingwood, who is one of those who calls the Bible unhistorical because it speaks of divine intervention, also says that the concept of the outworking of the divine

---

1. A. Berlin, *Poetics and Interpretation of Biblical Narrative* (Sheffield: Almond, 1983), 13 – 15, calls it a narrative representation.
2. See the useful discussion in Meir Sternberg, *The Poetics of Biblical Narrative* (Bloomington: Indiana Univ. Press, 1985), 23 – 35.
3. See R. G. Collingwood, *The Idea of History* (Oxford: Oxford Univ. Press, 1946), 11 – 12.

purpose is essential to history writing. Evidently he is thinking of the fact that there seem to be movements in history that are larger than the sum total of all the human choices involved. The human choices are significant, yet they do not seem to explain all that is happening.

Frankly, I think it is splitting hairs to distinguish between divine intervention and the outworking of divine purpose. Of course, one is direct and the other is indirect, but both involve a more than merely human factor in history. And if the Bible is correct that God does intervene, can truly accurate history avoid recording such interventions? To be sure, this assumes that there is privileged information explaining the true nature of the intervention and its meaning, and that is something that has proven difficult for children of the Enlightenment to accept. But I want to plead that we allow that possibility as we consider the nature of the documents.[4]

Of course, it must be asked whether the biblical reports are indeed accurate. What are we to make of miracles such as those at the exodus? What about the biblical use of numbers? What shall we conclude concerning the account of the conquest, especially in view of arguments today that there was no such thing? Is the Bible really fair with persons such as Ahab and Jezebel, whom the writers obviously consider to be detrimental to what Israel should be?

Ultimately, it will be difficult to find any truly unambiguous evidence to prove biblical accuracy on points such as these. What we must do is argue the question on other grounds. To begin with, we must ask the question that we asked concerning worldview. Whether the Bible is historically accurate or not, why does it differ so greatly from its neighboring cultures in its treatment of the past?

HISTORY AS REVELATION: INADEQUACIES

As mentioned in the introduction, arguments that the Bible is in some sense uniquely historical occasioned little objection fifty years ago. Thus, G. Ernest Wright could say, "The basis of the [biblical] literature was history, not nature, because the God of Israel was first of all the Lord of

---

4. A helpful discussion of the issues involved may be found in I. Provan et al., *A Biblical History of Israel* (Louisville: Westminster John Knox, 2003), 36–104.

history who used nature to accomplish his purposes in history."[5] Likewise, Gerhard von Rad said:

> But Israel also crossed the borderline [where historiography begins] and found her way to real historical writing, that most comprehensive form of a people's self-understanding to which in the whole of the ancient world, besides her, the Greeks alone found their way, and then along quite a different road.[6]

But the consensus represented in those two quotations was already beginning to break down in the 1960s. The only explanation scholars such as von Rad and Wright could give for Israel's thoroughgoing historical orientation was that God must have indeed acted in Israel's experience. But the majority of such scholars were also thoroughly committed to the historical-critical reconstruction of the Old Testament, which calls into question the validity of the Old Testament accounts of those acts. As a result there arose the formulation often attributed to Wright, but probably going behind him to his mentor, William F. Albright, that for the Bible *history is revelation*. That is, while the interpretations of God's actions to be found in the Bible are thoroughly human and, as such, deeply flawed, they do bear authentic witness to genuine actions of God, which were indeed revelatory.

Revelation Is Not Confined to Divine Action

However, it did not take long for other scholars to spot the flaws in that argument. As early as 1964, James Barr pointed out that the Bible does not understand revelation in such a way.[7] Much more frequently than it says, "The Lord did," it records that "The Lord said." Thus the Bible does not allow for a bifurcation between revelation and witness to revelation. Beyond that, Barr argued, if we accept that such a bifurcation does exist, then the "mighty acts of God" disappear. If we cannot trust the veracity of the reports of events, what do we know of the events? Historical inquiry

---

5. G. Ernest Wright, *The Old Testament against Its Environment* (London: SCM, 1950), 28.

6. Gerhard von Rad, *Old Testament Theology*, trans. D. M. G. Stalker (New York: Harper and Row, 1962), 1:52.

7. James Barr, "Revelation through History in the Old Testament and in Modern Theology," in *Interpretation* 17 (April 1963): 193–205.

is by nature skeptical and has only become more so in the twentieth and twenty-first centuries.

In fact, the *magnalia dei* ("the mighty acts of God") disappear, as B. Childs demonstrated in his *Biblical Theology in Crisis*.[8] If the only access we have to the revelatory acts of God is through a witness whose handling of "the facts" is almost everywhere agreed to be untrustworthy, we are forced to admit that we have no access to the "acts" at all. In a memorable line, Barr declared that "to consult the oracle of history is to raise the specter of Bultmann."[9] His point was that when we make Israel's history the basis of our faith, that history begins to erode before our eyes, and we are forced to "demythologize" the text, seeking some other basis for our faith than God's involvement in human-historical experience.

In making these points, Barr had no evangelical agenda. He pointed out these logical fallacies in order to remove the Bible from the category of historical revelation altogether. Not only did he not believe God acted, neither did he believe that God spoke. What we have in the Bible is not revelation at all. Instead, we have the religious speculation of the Hebrew people who have, somewhat unaccountably, chosen to use the vehicle of history instead of the vehicle of natural recurrences to convey their speculations.

As must be plain from what I have said previously, I disagree strongly with Barr's conclusions. However, I do agree that event and meaning cannot be separated. To that extent he offered a valuable corrective to what was ultimately a misguided attempt to save revelation from the hands of destructive criticism. Although the attempt was a worthwhile one, it was doomed from the start by its logical fallacy. If God did indeed intervene in Israel's life in order to reveal himself to the world, then the reports of the events and their interpretations must be as much revelation as the actions themselves, or the whole attempt would be fruitless.

Divine Action in History Is Not Unique to Israel

Another attack on the idea that the Bible's approach to history is unique appeared in 1967. In his *History and the Gods*, Bertil Albrektson questioned whether the idea that God is known as he acts in human history

---

8. B. Childs, *Biblical Theology in Crisis* (Philadelphia: Westminster, 1970).

9. Barr, "Revelation through History," 199. See further on this point below in ch. 8.

is all that distinctive.[10] In a careful analysis of ancient Near Eastern literature, he amassed a number of cases where one god or another is said to have acted in history on behalf of a client. On that point Albrektson's findings are quite convincing. From Amon-Re's intervention in the battle of Megiddo on Thutmoses III's behalf to Marduk's selection of Cyrus to bring Marduk back into Babylon, we can see the gods taking part in historic events. Furthermore, in the one or two "narrative histories," such as the Weidner Chronicle, we can see an overarching principle being used to evaluate behaviors.[11] Thus, if we were to say that what makes the Bible unique is the idea that God acts in history, that would surely be incorrect, and to the extent that the biblical theology movement's conceptual base rested on that assertion, Albrektson's work has been devastating.

However, I am *not* saying that the idea that God acts in history is what makes the Bible unique. The flaw in the biblical theology movement's conceptual structure was in its inability to accord the Bible's interpretations of the acts of God the same revelatory status as it gave to the acts themselves. As Barr pointed out, the Bible does not admit to such a distinction. It claims for the interpretations the same divine origin as for God's mighty acts. This is the point where the biblical uniqueness begins to assert itself. That one's deity could act in history was no new idea. But that this was the *only* place he acted that had significance for human beings, that those actions were according to a consistent, long-term purpose, that he was using the details of human-historical behavior to reveal that purpose, and that he was just as capable of using enemies as he was friends to accomplish his good purposes — that, I maintain, is not found anywhere else in the world, ancient or modern, outside of the Bible and its direct derivatives.[12] Thus,

---

10. B. Albrektson, *History and the Gods* (Lund: Gleerup, 1967).

11. In the case of the Weidner Chronicle the question is how persons have treated the temple of Marduk in Babylon. For a study see B. T. Arnold, "The Weidner Chronicle and the Idea of History in Israel and Mesopotamia," in *Faith, Tradition and History*, ed. A. Millard, J. Hoffmaier, and D. Baker (Winona Lake, IN: Eisenbrauns, 1994), 129 – 48.

12. It is the *combination* of these factors that defines the Bible's uniqueness. One or another of them can be found elsewhere in isolation. For instance, the Apology of Tukulti-Ninurta (B. Foster, *Before the Muses: An Anthology of Akkadian Literature* [Potomac, MD: CDL Press, 1996-], 1:209ff.) shows that others found it possible to think of a defeat at the hands of one's enemies to be a result of the displeasure of one's god.

the idea of God acting in history is not unique. But what Israel makes of that idea is unparalleled.

This idea was already to be found in von Rad's *Old Testament Theology*, where he writes: "This ability to deal with extensive complexes of connected history and not just episodes must be regarded as one of the most momentous advances in man's understanding of himself, since its effects upon the spiritual development of the whole of the West are incalculable."[13] Again he says:

> But the most important thing is that here Jahweh's action embraces every department of life, the wholly secular as well as the sacral — there is, in fact, a certain eagerness to discover it out in the secular world. It is only here that the belief — already latent in principle in the earliest Jahwism — that Jahweh is the cause of all things, finds its proper form. And, what is more, the chief sphere in which this action is exercised is the human heart.[14]

The same arguments addressed to Albrektson's point can be marshaled against H. W. F. Saggs, who, in his book *The Encounter with the Divine in Mesopotamia and Israel*, attempts to demonstrate that several of the concepts that have been attributed to the Bible as being unique were actually present in Mesopotamia as well.[15] In most cases his research is accurate. For instance, he shows that the Mesopotamians could conceive of a god as creator, in the sense that he is fully responsible for the world that is (though not in the biblical sense of creating something that had not existed in any form previously). Likewise he argues that it was possible for the Mesopotamians to think of deity as not being contained by this world. Whether that is truly transcendence or not, I am not certain, but that they could think in those terms I am fully ready to grant, in part, because my own studies have shown the same thing to be present in Egypt.

But what Saggs does not seem willing to grant is that the presence of these ideas in one form or another at one time or another does not mean that what they did with those ideas is identical to what Israel did with them.

---

13. Von Rad, *Old Testament Theology*, 1:50.

14. Ibid., 1:51.

15. H. W. F. Saggs, *The Encounter with the Divine in Mesopotamia and Israel* (London: Athlone, 1978).

Ultimately, this is where the difference lies. The Bible does not sometimes think of God as the sole Creator; it *always* thinks of him in that way. It never thinks of him in any other way. One can repeat this point on concept after concept; it is not that Israel is the only people who ever thought of an idea, it is that Israel is the first, and in most cases, the only culture to have carried that idea to its exclusive and logical conclusion.

Even more to the point, Israel is the only people to have combined a whole series of these ideas together in such a way as to come out at a radically different point than everybody else. They alone came to the conclusion that transcendence cannot coexist with continuity and followed out the implications of that decision in every area of life. This is clearly seen in the account of the golden calf. It seems clear that Aaron did not see himself as doing anything wrong in creating an idol of Yahweh. In the Egyptian milieu, it was possible to say that Amon-Re was beyond all things, including the gods, and *at the same time* physically present in the bull. Such an idea is at the heart of continuity thinking. Continuity does not rule out transcendence of a sort; it only rules out genuine transcendence. It was Moses who understood the real implications of the covenant stipulations, that the Creator of the universe is utterly discontinuous with his creation.[16]

NECESSITIES FOR HISTORY WRITING FOUND IN ISRAEL

R. G. Collingwood concludes that the Bible contains no historical writing. He does so largely on the grounds of divine intervention. However, when he defines the concepts that he considers essential to historical writing he finds that all have their roots in the New Testament. Those concepts are:

1. Sin causing non-achievement of goals
2. Denial of eternal entities

---

16. J. Oswalt, "The Golden Calves and the Egyptian Concept of Deity," *Evangelical Quarterly* 45 (1974): 13–20. In the above paragraph, I have referred to "Israel" as having these concepts and maintaining them consistently. Clearly that is not the case in any absolute sense. The Bible is clear that in historical Israel, there was a wide variety of beliefs and practices, from outright paganism to a rather paganized Yahwism to exclusive Yahwism. It is in Israel's Bible that the astonishing consistency is seen.

3. Disinterested providence (no favorites)
4. Outworking of divine purposes in history
5. Apocalypse
6. Periods
7. Universalism[17]

(1) The first of these is important because it raises the issue of a standard outside of mere efficiency in evaluating the ultimate value of choices and events. Was the decision "right" or "wrong" on some higher level than mere utility? (2) The second is addressed particularly to the denial of eternal good and eternal evil as hidden forces that actually direct all events apart from human choices and decisions. (3) With regard to disinterested providence, Collingwood suggests that history writing cannot exist where there are heroes "who can do no wrong." There must be a standard over and above the hero. (4) The idea of the outworking of divine purposes, as mentioned above, contributes to the necessary recognition in history writing that the whole of history is more than merely the sum of its parts. One can see a sweep in human events that is larger than a simple listing of the choices involved might indicate.

(5) Apocalypse teaches us that there is a forward movement in human history, and that this movement is leading toward definable ends. (6) Coupled directly to that idea of forward movement toward an end is the idea of periods. As one looks at the movement of history, it is possible to define stages along the way, each of which contributes in some way toward the overall movement. (7) Finally, there is universalism, that is, the view that this is one world and that all of its events can be understood according to a single set of standards.

What is surprising to me is Collingwood's failure to see that these are as much characteristics of the Old Testament as they are the New. Furthermore, he does not seem to see that apart from the common worldview that the two Testaments share, in contrast to everyone else, none of those concepts would exist. It is the Bible's insistence that there is one transcendent God, who is utterly consistent in character and purpose, apart from whom nothing else exists, that gives rise to the concepts that are essential

---

17. Collingwood, *History*, 46–52.

to history writing.[18] Furthermore, the Bible insists that Yahweh has made all this known through human-historical experience. That being so, why would we say that the reporting of his actions and words therefore disqualifies the resulting accounts from being historically accurate?

All of this leads us to the question of the reason for the recording of these historical experiences. Surely the reason is so that God can be known. If it is in the unique events of time and space that God is revealed, then those events — and their divinely mediated interpretations — must be recorded. If he were to be known in the vast natural recurrences, then careful recording would hardly be necessary — we will see them all again. But if he is known by means of unique, nonrecurring events, those must be remembered. Beyond that, since this God, unlike the pagan gods, is characterized by faithfulness, it is necessary to report those events faithfully. Falsifying them can hardly lead to true reflection on them.[19] This is only fortified by the fact that the transcendent One stands outside of the record, judging and evaluating the recorder. There is a consistent standard that not only calls kings to account, but also court reporters.

To me all this argues for the accuracy of the historical reporting. The conceptual differences between the Bible's approach to history and that of the other cultures are real. And these conceptual differences result in some very different forms and functions. John Walton has tabulated these differences in a helpful way:

1. The biblical treatment of the past is theological and didactic; the ancient Near East's use of the past is propagandistic.
2. The biblical material is found in a single corpus with a unified purpose; there is nothing similar in the ancient Near East.

---

18. This statement could well give rise to the question, "Then how do you explain Thucydides and Herodotus? They certainly did not have the benefit of the biblical worldview." As von Rad said in the quotation above, they came by a very different road. That road was the Greek philosophers, who intuited a "universe" and to a large extent "demythologized" it. In so doing they arrived at several of Collingwood's essential concepts. However, in the end the philosophers were not able to find an adequate basis for their intuitions, and Greek thought fell back into a mythological polytheism. As it did so, Greek history writing disappeared. See the discussion in ch. 1.
19. This does not presume some modern, Western preoccupation with exactitude. But it does mean that there is a bar against intentionally altering the report for any of number of "good" reasons.

3. In the Bible divine intervention is toward an established and consistent goal; in ancient Near Eastern literature there is no overall plan.
4. In the Bible the concepts of election and covenant provide a framework for understanding human-historical experience.
5. The prevalence of omen texts in the ancient Near East demonstrates the conviction that existence is profoundly cyclical; there is nothing to suggest this in the Bible.[20]

Thus, as was the case with myth, we can find a number of similarities in detail between the Bible's view of human experience and that of Israel's neighbors. But when we look at the way in which those details are incorporated, we find a whole that is essentially different. A different way of viewing reality has resulted in a different way of looking at, evaluating, and recording human experience, one with no comparison elsewhere in its own day and in days to come.

So in the Bible, history, a matter of rather minor concern in the ancient Near Eastern literatures, comes to have an importance out of proportion to anything found elsewhere. Nor are the differences only a matter of degree of attention. The biblical writers, rightly or wrongly, clearly believe that decisions of ultimate importance are made in this world and that if God is to be found anywhere, it is here.

This concept, of course, comes to its clearest expression in the incarnation. In Christ it is made plain what the Old Testament had been saying all along: since we humans are incapable of going out of the world to find God, God has come to us, and in so doing he has bestowed on this world, its people, and events a significance and a reality they could never have had otherwise. The incarnation was not a "sport," a "one-off" event. It was the logical continuation of what had been taking place since the beginning of the human race.

What Are the Origins of Israel's Unique Understanding?

Where did this approach come from? Did Israel follow the same thought processes as did its neighbors? Did it too start by speculating on the given?

---

20. J. Walton, *Ancient Israelite Literature in Its Cultural Context* (Grand Rapids: Zondervan, 1989), 233–34.

If so, then why did they alone come out at a radically different endpoint? It was popular in the late 1800s, when Israel's religion was considered to be the highest achievement in the human religious quest, to speak of the Hebrew religious genius. Shall we turn to that here? Shall we explain Israel's grasp of the transcendent God who reveals himself in the context of unique human experiences as an expression of some unusual facilities of perception?

No, it will not do. If genius is the key, then there is no reason for Israel to have made these unique discoveries. Pride of place would have to go to the Sumerians or the Old Kingdom Egyptians. Here were the real cognitive and cultural geniuses of the ancient Near East. Their discoveries shaped the thinking, commerce, politics, and science of the whole region for almost three thousand years. In fact, we still today use the Sumerians' sexagesimal mathematics when we divide a circle into 360 degrees. Yet when it came to their perception of ultimate reality, these profound thinkers came out where they started. If the given is this world and if any outside interpretation of that given is rejected, the final conclusions are all going to be the same — namely, those detailed in the earlier chapters.

So if the Hebrews came out with different — radically different — conclusions about the nature of reality and the nature of human experience, they did so because they started somewhere different from everybody else. They, of course, tell us where that point was. It was in direct revelation from the transcendent One himself. Unlike the Greeks, who were willing to accept the accolades of being the world's greatest thinkers, the Israelites tell us that they were religiously retarded. Far from claiming to be unusually sensitive to religious truth, they tell us again and again that they were stubborn and stiff-necked, a people afflicted with severe spiritual myopia.

Nor is this merely false modesty. Their whole history is one of failure after another to live up to the light recorded in their own literature. Thus, we are forced to pay serious attention to the Hebrews' claims to have gotten their views by special revelation. No other explanation fits the circumstances. Their view of God and of the world is unparalleled elsewhere. If they did not get it from the source they claim, no other good candidates present themselves.

Revelation through Human-Historical Experience Calls for Careful Recording

Now if this revelation came to them through their history, as they claim, it only heightens the earlier argument about the recorders having done their job with special care. To have done otherwise would be for them to deny the very understanding that was informing their task. What does this mean about the accuracy of the history of the Bible? It argues for a high degree of accuracy. If God is not history and yet is revealed through history as divinely interpreted, it was of the greatest importance to record accurately what happened and to report as precisely as possible what God said about the meaning of what happened. To falsify the record or the interpretation was to be left with nothing that was of any value for knowing God or for making sense out of one's life.

But what do we mean by accuracy? Again, I would not want to claim that the Bible's history writing is on a par with modern history writing, particularly in the attempt of modern history writing to be exhaustive and complete. John Walton has classified history writing under eight different headings. Of these, "journalistic" and "academic" would most clearly define modern historiography, and he rightly says that there was nothing like those concerns for eyewitness reporting in either Israel or anywhere else in the ancient world.[21] Clearly, that is not a part of the Bible's intent.

Thus, I would not argue that we can use the biblical accounts to reconstruct exactly what happened in this or that instance. Thoughtful readers may well differ on what the actual event might have looked like in a given instance. But clearly it is not the Bible's intent to give us eyewitness accounts in most cases, and one of the things modern interpretation has rightly stressed is that we should interpret any text from the standpoint of its own genre and intentions (unless we opt for deconstructionism, which then means anything goes). Clearly, when the Bible reports on and interprets a human-historical experience, its main concern is with the meaning of that experience. The details are important, but only insofar as they help us to grasp that meaning. This is not to suggest that the details can be

---

21. John H. Walton, *Ancient Near Eastern Thought and the Old Testament* (Grand Rapids: Baker, 2006), 231.

rearranged to suit the predilections of the writer (or the reader), but only that reproducing a complete picture is not of first interest.[22]

What this means is that while two readers of an account might reconstruct the experience reported somewhat differently, if they were treated to an "instant replay" of the experience[23] and looked at the report of it in the text, they would agree that, yes, that is indeed what happened. Thus, we have by no means a complete account of the exodus from Egypt, but there is good reason to believe that what is reported is fully accurate as far as it goes. That is, by means of historical writing we the readers can enter into that experience and in so doing encounter Yahweh in the same way that the Hebrews were able to encounter him. We are able to participate in the experience to the degree that we are prepared to receive the same interpretation that they received and to draw the proper conclusions from it.

To this extent, the accuracy of the reporting is of vital importance. The religious interpretations did not create the "historical" accounts. Rather, God's interventions in human life were the basis for the inspired interpretations that challenged everything that Israel had learned during its four-hundred-year sojourn in what was arguably the most thoroughgoing expression of the worldview of continuity in the world at that time. The Bible reports to us that they broke away from both Egyptian bondage and from the Egyptian understanding of the world because of unique, nonrepeatable experiences that were divinely interpreted to them. If that was not the case, we are hard-pressed to explain why Israel chose to create this unique historical fiction to tell its story.

The above statements may well open me to the charge that I have fallen prey to "the empiricist fallacy," namely, that I have made the validity of the faith subject to whether its basis can be empirically proven or not. I do

---

22. Baruch Halpern says that a historian must be concerned with telling the truth about what happened within the limits of his or her knowledge and ability; see "The State of Israelite History," in *Reconsidering Israel and Judah: Recent Studies on the Deuteronomistic History,* ed. G. Knoppers and J. G. McConville (Winona Lake, IN: Eisenbrauns, 2000), 562. To do so, he says, the historian may reconstruct speeches, for instance, that were not actually made, but which from the historian's perspective give a true perspective of the issues.

23. My use of "experience" here is intentional. We cannot abstract the "exodus event" from all that the text gives us by way of interpretation. The interpretation was as much a part of the whole as were the plagues and the crossing of the sea.

not think that is the case. It seems to me that there are two extremes to be avoided in this discussion. On the one hand, if we say that none of the experiences recorded in the Bible took place, or if they did, they occurred in ways completely different from the way they are described in the text, then the theological interpretations given to those occurrences are inexplicable, as I have sought to show above. That is one extreme.

The other extreme is to say that the basis of our faith is in certain historic events and that unless the events took place "exactly" as reported in the text, we cannot believe the biblical theology. No, our faith is in the God who revealed himself in the context of Israel's historical experience. That experience involved persons and events, and interpretations of those persons and events. The validity of the interpretations cannot be separated from the facticity of the persons and the events, but facticity is no guarantee of the validity of the interpretations. Thus, if Israel did not experience a miraculous crossing of a body of water in its escape from Egypt, its claims to be the chosen people of God are highly suspect, but accepting that conviction does not require us to find absolute proof of the precise details of the crossing.

CHAPTER 8

DOES IT MATTER WHETHER THE BIBLE IS HISTORICAL? THE PROBLEM OF HISTORY (2)

The previous chapter closed with the argument that since theology and interpretation and divine activity in the realm of human-historical experience are inseparable from one another, the historical accuracy of the accounts is a matter of importance. But is that really true? In the end, does it really matter whether Israel's historical experiences (1) actually occurred, (2) are accurately reported, and (3) are correctly interpreted? Suppose we learn in one way or another that the experiences reported in the Bible did not actually occur, as is not infrequently argued today. Is anything really lost?[1] After all, large blocks of the Old Testament are not "historical" at all; the poetic and wisdom literature is not, and in the Prophets history is only tangential at best, with prophetic oracles taking the center stage. Why not simply draw back our lines of defense and grant the possibility that the narrative substructure of the Old Testament, and of the Gospels as well, is only a vehicle designed to convey a somewhat distinctive faith perspective?

So we could argue that the German distinction between *Historie* and *Geschichte* is a valid one here. *Historie* defines what happened and is the domain of the historian. *Geschichte* tell us what was going on and is the domain of the theologian. Ultimately, it is not the facts of outer history that matter but the inner reality, wherein lies the true meaning of things. Here is the point of James Barr's remark about Bultmann: if we link our faith too closely to historic fact, we may discover that those historic facts have

---

1. The question was famously expressed in G. W. Ramsey's *The Quest for Historical Israel* (Atlanta: John Knox, 1981), in the chapter title, "If Jericho Was Not Razed, Is Our Faith in Vain?" 107.

disappeared and we are thus left with nothing. Better to separate faith from fact and thus be left with something, whatever that may be.

The Entire Bible Is "Historical"

How should we respond to these proposals? First of all, we can readily admit that the Bible is much more than a recital of historical facts. It is even more than historical narrative. But can the biblical message, whether Old Testament or New, be abstracted from its historical substructure? I maintain that it cannot be, and I will demonstrate below that attempts to do so ultimately fall short. The Bible refuses to allow us to create a split between fact and meaning. In fact, the entire Bible is historical in that in its entirety it is an interpretation of the historical experience of Israel culminating in the life, death, and resurrection of Christ.

Thus, the speech of God is never in the air. It is always in relation to what someone is experiencing. Think of God's speeches in the Pentateuch, where he says what he says in the context of human experiences, from the fall in Genesis 3 to the Plains of Moab in Deuteronomy 34. The same is true for the Prophets. Yahweh's oracles through the prophets are largely meaningless unless we know the historical context in which they spoke. Thus, their words are historical words because everything the prophets have to say is in the light of the historical Israel and her covenant with Yahweh.

On this point it is hardly accidental that the second section of the Hebrew canon, the Nebiʾim ("the Prophets"), begins with Joshua, Judges, Samuel, and Kings and only then goes on to Isaiah, Jeremiah, Ezekiel, and the Twelve. By grouping its authoritative books in that way, the Israelite community was recognizing that "history" is unintelligible apart from the prophets, and that the ministry of the prophets was squarely within the context of Israel's experience. Thus, the Septuagint did us something of a disservice in separating "books of history" from "books of prophecy," because it allowed us to imagine that historical experience and prophecy really can be separated in Israel.

So also the poetic books, as part of the canon, are a reflection on Israel's life with the God of the fathers, who was revealed to them in their historical experience as Yahweh. Why do Israel's psalms, which at their lowest level overlap Canaanite expressions, at their highest level rise from that point to something radically different from anything else in ancient Near Eastern hymnic literature? What explanation would the Israelites give? Surely they would say to us, "Ah, this is the Yahweh who has revealed himself to us in our historic experience." By no means would they say to us, "Well, we have a certain genius for doing praise in fresh ways." It is Israel's unique experience of Yahweh in the context of unique experiences in time and space that accounts for the book of Psalms.

Nor is the case different with the Israelite wisdom literature. While we may recognize the clear similarities between the biblical wisdom literature and wisdom literature from the ancient Near Eastern world, whether optimistic or pessimistic, we must equally recognize that the biblical wisdom literature still comes out at a different place. Why is it that in the Bible the highest wisdom is to fear God and obey his commandments? Why is it that foolishness is wickedness (not simply stupidity), and wisdom is righteousness (not merely shrewdness)? Where does accumulated human experience lead to those conclusions outside of Israel?

I suspect that the biblical wisdom literature is the result of an experiment, which went something like this: "Given what we have learned about the nature of reality through Yahweh's revelation to us, what does that do to the wisdom of the world? If Yahweh is the Creator of the world, it would seem as though what wise and thoughtful people have learned about what works in the world, and what doesn't, would at least be consistent with what he has shown us." In other words, no less than the rest of the Bible the wisdom literature is also shaped by Israel's historical experience. God redeems and judges in history; his will is made known in history, and it must be lived out in history. Nature is not the grid through which God is experienced, worshiped, and obeyed; human-historical experience is.

Thus, to suggest that what actually happened to Israel is of little moment, either in understanding what they believed, why they believed it, or what the significance of that belief is for us, is to create a non sequitur. It is to say that the conclusions of the argument have no necessary relation to the premises on which that argument is based, or that the conclusions may be considered valid although they are actually derived from very different premises than those stated. Any attempt to make revelation or inspiration an inner psychic experience removed from historic verification must founder on Scripture's own claims: you should believe what we say because what we say grows out of things that actually happened.

ARE BIBLICAL FAITH AND BIBLICAL HISTORY REALLY INSEPARABLE?

But again, we come to the question with which the chapter began. Are biblical *faith* and biblical *history* really inseparable? Is it not possible to maintain the biblical faith even if it is cut loose from the activity of God in history as reported in the Bible? There have been two notable attempts to do so, and I want to explore each of them briefly. They are the work of Rudolf Bultmann and the development of the thought of Alfred North Whitehead now called process theology. Each of them attempts to take "history" seriously as it relates to Christian theology, but each of them starts from the premise that what the Bible records as history is not accurate and that indeed such accuracy is a matter of little significance. Thus, they each in different ways seek to recognize the Bible's distinctive emphasis on history while avoiding what is to them the quagmire of verifiability.[2]

The Bultmannian Approach

The Existentialist Foundation

As is well known, Rudolf Bultmann sought to use existentialist philosophy as a base from which to address the problem of history in biblical faith.[3] This philosophy (which continues to undergird much of what is

---

2. It may be thought presumptuous of me to attempt to summarize, much less respond to, such great bodies of thought in such a short compass. Nevertheless, I do believe it should be possible to treat great ideas fairly in a brief space. If I have misunderstood what either or both are saying, that is another matter, but it does not have to do with brevity.

3. While Bultmann's work focused on the New Testament, I include a treatment of him here because he is a prime example of the attempt to extricate "history" from "myth." Some of his more important works are: *Primitive Christianity in Its Contemporary Setting*, trans. R. H. Fuller (London: Collins, 1960); *Theology of the New Testament*, trans. K. Grobel (New York: Scribners, 1951–1955); *History and Eschatology* (Edinburgh: University Press, 1957); *The Gospel of John: A Commentary*, trans. G. Beasley-Murray (Oxford: Blackwell, 1971). See also *Kerygma and Myth: A Theological Debate*, ed. H.-W. Bartsch, trans. R. H. Fuller (London: SPCK, 1972).

called "postmodern" thought today) was a radical call to action — the action of taking responsibility for one's own existence. Instead of seeing the self as an entity shaped by history and a human "nature," this way of thinking sees "existence" as the most fundamental aspect of historic consciousness. One's existence in each moment is reality; that moment has no necessary predecessor or any necessary successor. The result is a radical openness and a radical freedom. Ultimately, there is no experience of history that "means" anything concrete.

In such a situation, if a human being wishes to "exist" and not merely "live," he or she will have to choose to do so.[4] This is in the nature of a forced choice, much like that which a person might face being in the back seat of a car speeding out of control downhill toward a steep cliff at the bottom. Failure to choose to jump is itself a choice to die. Only the person who has openly faced the nausea of meaninglessness and has freely chosen to give his or her life meaning in some way can be said to be living authentically, truly "existing." This makes history a *part* of one's consciousness rather than the *determiner* of one's experiences.

The Problem of History

In attempting to construct his theology Bultmann recognizes two problems. The first is philosophical and lies in the ambiguity of the term "history." How is it possible to speak of "objective facts of history" at all? In existentialist thought there is no situation outside of the immediacy of consciousness from which we could ever hope to gain a perspective by which to determine absolutely what is subjective and what is objective. All narratives are dependent on the mind of the interpreter. To the extent that "objectivity" means anything at all, it is a scientific term, relating to weights and measures. But "history" is an art — indeed, a statement of faith. And even if it were possible to produce an objective record of events in the past, would they have any *meaning* for *me*, now, anyway? Those things are gone, never to be repeated. If one were to allow them to have a determinative effect on the present moment of existence, this would be to refuse the existential demand for authenticity. It is now that a person must choose to exist.

---

4. The reader will note that this is a reversal of the connotations given these words in popular English. The usage here reflects the German connotations.

Coupled with the problem of the ambiguity of history is the supposed decimation of biblical history by the critical studies of the past century. According to these studies many of the biblical "events" never occurred, particularly those of a "metaphysical" (or miraculous) nature, which "history" teaches us cannot occur. Thus, a truly "scientific" record of Israel's development or of Jesus' life would look very different from the accounts we have in the Bible. Even if the said events might have occurred — as events — they do not "mean" what the Bible says they do.

All of this means that the entanglement of biblical theology with these faulty "historical" statements is a serious problem for the contemporary believer. So what shall we do? Shall we dismiss the New Testament along with the Old?[5] Is the Bible merely an example of a prescientific stage in human thinking, which we have now surpassed? No, we cannot do that, says Bultmann. The reason we cannot is that the Bible (the New Testament) seems to be categorically different from other books. Somehow in this book more than any other we find God confronting us, defining our existential choices in a uniquely penetrating way.

This poses a dilemma for us: as a historical record the Bible is not merely inaccurate according to the critics, it is patently false; yet, as a word of God's judgment upon, and redemption of, a sinful world, it speaks with authority. What is to be done, since especially in the Gospels, the authoritative Word and the faulty history would seem to be part and parcel of each other? How can the validity of the Divine Word be maintained?

Distinguishing Historie from Geschichte

For Bultmann the answer is to be found in a separation of the narrative (*Geschichte*) from the event (*Historie*). As mentioned above, *Historie* defines what happened and is the domain of the historian. *Geschichte* tells us what was going on and is the domain of the theologian.[6] These two different

---

5. It is precisely because it is so much more difficult to disentangle Old Testament theology from Old Testament "history" than is true in the New Testament that Bultmann straightforwardly dismisses the Old Testament as the Word of God.

6. It is interesting to speculate on the impact of this German vocabulary on Immanuel Kant's thinking, because his distinction between fact and meaning, and ultimately between reason and pure reason, seems to lie right at this point.

terms seem to make it possible to draw an intellectual distinction between event and interpretation, and that seems to make it possible to retrieve the content of scriptural theology from the dead hand of the historical critic.

This distinction between narrative and event makes possible the following statement, which is typically Bultmannian: any attempt to imprison the Divine in *Historie* is distinctly unhistorical (*ungeschichtliche*)(!).[7] Why is this true? Because *Historie* shows that humans are utterly responsible for themselves and their world. Thus, any attempt to mix human and divine cannot be speaking "historically" but rather must be speaking "metaphysically." Thus, to speak of Jesus as having both a human and a divine nature is, by definition (for Bultmann), to be speaking "metaphysically." *Historie*, as defined by Bultmann, cannot admit such a possibility.

So what would a "historic" account of Jesus look like (and, by extension, a historic account of Israel)? Well, history (in an existentialist understanding) teaches us (*Geschichte*) that humans are utterly free and responsible in the light of the past and the hope of the future. That is, our choices are absolutely unconditioned by anything, and we, if we are to be something other than a cow, must stand up and take responsibility for our choices.[8] Where the hope is in this is somewhat difficult to ascertain, but perhaps it is the hope that our choices will turn out for the "good" in the future. But in classic existentialism, it is difficult to determine exactly what that "good" is.

At any rate, a historic (*geschichtliche*) account of Jesus would stress his free and responsible obedience to God and his acceptance of responsibility for the world in eternity. We see a Jesus who freely accepts an unjust cross

---

7. Note that both German terms are translated by the English word "history." So the sense of the statement is that to imprison God in facts is a historical misinterpretation. It makes the narrative say something that is manifestly impossible. I will comment below on this characteristically "slippery" use of language.

8. This has certain overtones of Greek tragedy. The difference is that in the Greek drama the hero did not have a real choice, his or her choice having been conditioned by fate. But the issue of acceptance of responsibility is the point of similarity. We the spectators are ennobled when we see the hero or heroine nobly accepting responsibility for their (conditioned) choice and not limply claiming "it wasn't my fault." Existentialism says it was my choice and I will take the consequences. A good statement of these themes in novelistic form may be found in *The Stranger* by Albert Camus. But it should be noted that existentialist thinking is by no means monolithic: Sartre's representation of it is not identical to that of Camus.

as the result of his choice to stand against the inauthentic choices of the religious elites of his day, who followed "historically" defined conventions. Thus, he shows the way of new life to all who will follow in his footsteps. These followers, having rejected the sin of living in bondage to the "world," as he did, will not be defeated by death any more than he was.

So if this is the meaning of the message of Christ, how shall we explain the "metaphysical" presentation of Jesus in the Gospels, the entanglement of the Christ of faith with the Jesus of supposed historical event? Why the stress on the physical and miraculous events of Jesus' ministry? For Bultmann, working especially on the basis of the gospel of John, the "metaphysical" language of the Bible was a gnostic "parable" designed to both conceal and reveal the mystery of Christ Jesus. The *cognoscenti*, the elect, were able to penetrate beyond the husk to the real message revealed within the "parable," whereas the *non-cognoscenti*, those who were judged unworthy, only saw the fantastic details of the accounts and were never able to get beyond them.

At the time, in a prescientific age where the miraculous was (supposedly) a part of everyday life, such a "parabolic" presentation was perfectly justified, and indeed the "metaphysical" presentation was a help to the understanding of the elect. However, today, in a world "come of age," where it is understood that no such ruptures in the fabric of time and space are possible, the "parable" has become a positive hindrance to our hearing of the message of the "historic" Jesus. Thus, it is time for us to discard the "old wineskin" of the "metaphysical" language and to extract the eternal Word from its stifling metaphysical (supernatural) garb, clothing it in new historic (human) terms.

Denying the Subject-Object Distinction

But beyond the hindrance which the "metaphysical" mingling of *Historie* and *Geschichte* poses, there is a further reason to remove the Word from *Historie*. That is that *Historie* has fallen prey to the scientific misconception of a distinction between subject and object. To assume the possibility of such a distinction is to imagine that there can be something from which I, the subject, am utterly detached: an object. I study it without any personal interest in the outcome of my study, or without any personal concern for it as an object.

Thus, to make God or Christ an "object" of study (e.g., historical inquiry) is "idolatrous." That is, I have made God a thing to be studied, even to be manipulated. For Bultmann, even to have a worldview is to make the world an idol. Life is to be experienced, to be lived, to be filled with authentic choices. To reduce it to concepts that can be categorized and pigeon-holed is to have chosen to live inauthentically. So it is also with God. God is the eternal Subject — never to be contained, never to be caught and examined like an amoeba in a test tube. To seek to verify miracles is to accept the reality criteria of the "natural" man and thus to turn God, the eternal Subject, into an object.

In the end, then, not only do we not *need* to concern ourselves with the accuracy of the historical accounts in the Bible, we *must* not so concern ourselves. To do so would be to fly in the very face of what the text is trying to do. It would be as though in order to subject a container to study as an object, we poured its precious contents out onto the ground and forgot them. In truth, we should forget the container; it has no bearing on the nature of the contents. It is not the metaphysical container but the Verbal Reality — the *kerygma*, that is, the contents — that must claim our attention.

Critique

How shall we respond to this presentation? At the outset we must appreciate the seriousness and the sincerity of Bultmann's concern. Although modern Western culture has become thoroughly enmeshed in its rationalism, individualism, and historicism, Bultmann is unwilling to allow the biblical message to fall prey to these, but is seeking to find a way to make that message accessible to those for whom these elements are a given. One must also admire the deft way in which he succeeded in adapting the tenets of existentialism to those of Christian faith, although perhaps in the end we will conclude that the adaptation went in the other direction.

Secondary issues. But despite Bultmann's seriousness and sincerity, he did not succeed in "saving the faith" by separating the Verbal Reality from its container. I will begin with two of what I judge to be lesser issues before moving on to those that I think are more destructive to his effort. The first of these secondary issues is that he seems to privilege the modern interpreter in relation to the text. At the same time, he allows a modern construct, scientific empiricism, to have controlling impact on the reading. Thus, Bultmann and the modern interpreter are put in a position to decide what is mere vehicle, or container, and what is not according to certain philosophical a prioris, such as that *Historie* can only concern humans. It could be charged that any interpreter, including the conservative interpreter, does as much, determining what is essential to the meaning of the text and what is not. But whether they have always succeeded or not, conservatives have at least attempted to interpret the text within its own categories, not those of an alien philosophical system. Using that system, Bultmann devises new categories for what is meaningful in the text and what is not.

A second somewhat minor issue is his ambiguous use of words. This is a particular defect in a method whose purpose is to clarify essential meanings. However, it is unfortunately characteristic of existentialism. This philosophy seems to pursue a gnosticism of its own, using everyday terms in ways that only the "elect" will understand. So when Bultmann speaks of Christianity as a "historic" religion, he means something radically different from the common understanding of that statement. He does not mean that Christianity's theology grows out of God's intersection with humans in their historical experiences, as was understood for nearly two millennia. He only means that it emphasizes, in his terms, radical choice and responsibility for that choice. Another example is in his labeling of descriptions of the miracles that occur in time and space (and nowhere else) as "metaphysical." This is certainly not the way "metaphysical" has been used historically.

Yet another instance of this ambiguous use of words is the contradiction involved in his phrase "Verbal Reality." In the nature of the case a "word" is a symbol for a reality standing behind it. In our language words function as symbols that have referents. The referent to which the symbol points, however, is distinct from the symbol. That means that words only have meaning in relation to the items to which they refer.[9] Words (and ideas) carry with them an inherent "aboutness." If the word is a container that carries a message (the entity or concept), then the container and the message are not so easily separated as Bultmann thinks. Here he shows his

---

9. To state this point more precisely, the epistemic value of a word is rooted in an ontological relation it has to the entity or concept that it represents.

gnostic hand most clearly: the symbol is its own reality. He has therefore not only redefined the faith, but also the nature of language.

More serious issues. But beyond these issues are ones that are even more serious in my mind. First is the fact that Bultmann virtually removes God from the natural order of reality. God is only accessible in "inner-personal" encounter. In that case, the real question is whether God exists at all. If I only know something within myself, and it is not susceptible to demonstration in some way outside of my own psyche, what is that knowledge but subjective delusion? In response to this, Bultmann would immediately reply that in my searching for confirmation outside of myself, I have fallen prey to the false subject-object distinction. That is, to objectify anything is to fail to realize that any thought we have is only a thought *in* my thought as the thinking subject. It is to fail to recognize my own responsibility for, and to, this "object" of my consciousness. But here the existentialist fails to recognize that a thought about God is *in reference* to something that is beyond my own mind. To deny the subject-object distinction is to retreat into a philosophical conundrum whereby one can define reality entirely in terms of one's own thinking.

Whatever we may make of European philosophy's three-hundred-year struggle to define reality, the plain fact is that my personal thoughts about something do not make it a reality. As I said above, I may believe with all my heart that I am Napoleon, but my subjective conviction will not make it so. I may choose (in existential terms) to *be* Napoleon, and I may indeed give my life meaning on that basis, but the fact of the matter is that my belief will not overcome the historic distinction between the French emperor and me. If something is not so, no amount of belief will make it so. Thus, for the Bible, faith is not a Kierkegaardian leap into the dark. Rather, it is a considered step into space on the basis of sufficient evidence outside of one's own belief.[10]

---

10. In his *God Is There and He Is Not Silent* (Wheaton, IL: Tyndale, 1972), 99 – 100, Francis Schaeffer offered a helpful analogy. A climber in the Alps late in the day is suddenly enveloped in cold, blustery clouds. Knowing that he is on a narrow trail on the side of a cliff, he is afraid to go forward or back. At the same time, he knows he cannot remain in that exposed place through the night, for he will die of cold and damp. But suddenly, he hears a voice out of the fog telling him to get down and lower himself off the trail, hanging

This relegation of God to the inner world of private conviction had a predictable result. That result was the "God is dead" movement of the 1970s and later. The "metaphysical" God of the Bible who can act in the identifiable world of time and space is indeed dead. There is no such God. Any "encounter" with "God" is purely interior and is by definition unverifiable. This is only intensified by the strident individualism of existentialism. The bridge between the outer world of *Historie* and the inner world of *Geschichte* has been completely destroyed. The result is that the "Verbal Reality" of God is utterly separate from the life of the community, which is finally what gives meaning and substance to daily life. If "God" is irrelevant to vibrant community life, and if community life is all that makes life worth living, then that mental "counter-God" has no necessary function in the world and can be dispensed with. Far from having saved the biblical God by cutting him loose from history, Bultmann actually succeeded in destroying him.

Another deeply serious flaw in Bultmann's thinking is his faulty conception of history. In every ordinary definition of the term, "history" has to do with the past. Yet, Bultmann's conception of what is truly historical specifically excludes the past. The past is dead to us, meaningless, in the sense that it in no way shapes what is happening now. Likewise, the future is completely unconditioned by either the past or the present. To be sure, we may *choose* to relate these, but they have no *necessary* relationship to each other. In fact, it is only what is occurring now that is significant. Only as

---

from the edge by his fingers, feeling nothing under his feet. But when he lets go, the voice says, he will only drop a foot or two onto a ledge where there is a cave that he can get into out of the wind until morning. Now, Schaeffer says, if the climber actually does that, he is not exercising faith, but is a fool. But suppose he calls back and asks who the mysterious speaker is, and the speaker identifies himself as one of the foremost Alpine guides in the area. The climber asks where the speaker is, and hears that he is on another mountain just across the deep gulf separating it from the climber's mountain. The climber asks if the speaker really does know the situation as well as he claims, and the speaker tells the climber that a few feet ahead of him is a distinctive rock outcropping with a tiny stunted tree growing out of it, and when the climber checks, he finds it just as the speaker said. Now, says Schaeffer, if the climber gets down and hangs off the edge of the trail by his fingers, he will still feel nothing under his feet. But to let go now is an act of faith and not of folly. This is what the Bible is offering us in the evidence of history, but that is precisely the kind of "objective" verification that Bultmann disdains, calling it an act of idolatry.

I choose now to participate in the eternal crucifixion (not the crucifixion of *Historie*, but the crucifixion of *Geschichte*) does that "event" have any meaning. It is only as I decide to choose now, accepting the indeterminate consequences of that choice, that I can be said to be living historically.

In fact, this understanding of reality is similar to that of myth. There is no real connection between the situation of the present and the choices of the past. It is the eternal, not-time-conditioned "activity" of the divine that has significance for "now." If I choose to replicate this activity, I will be fulfilling my destiny. But my choices in the "now" do not have any necessary bearing on the future; I have no real say in the shaping of what takes place tomorrow. I can only take whatever may come to me as a result of my choices and try to endure such events in a noble way. Thus in the end, there is no existence except what is in the present, and the only reality is the inner reality of my own choosing. By what right, I ask, can such an understanding be called "historical"? It is the very opposite of all that has been thought of as having to do with "history."

A truly historical conception of reality attempts to record the affairs of humans honestly in view of an overarching standard of evaluation that is rooted in the supposed nature of things. It does so because that reality stands apart from the one recording the events — and from the events themselves. It concludes that the effects of the acts of humans in time and space can be traced forward in concatenations that are genuinely different from those out of which they emerged. Thus, it becomes possible to discern whether there is progress or regress in the directions of human life. Furthermore, on the basis of an overarching standard of evaluation, it becomes possible to predict outcomes of given actions, which become the foundation of shared human experience. This idea, which is foreign to both the ancient and the modern mind, is native to the Bible.

In summary, Rudolf Bultmann's solution to the problem of history and biblical faith was, and is, a failure. His attempt to preserve the validity of the Word while discarding its outmoded wineskin in which a transcendent God acts in the world of time and space not only does not work, but it actually plays into that understanding of reality that the Bible specifically sets itself to contradict. In short, the biblical understanding of reality cannot be separated from its historic rootage.

Process Thought

Although the proponents of what is now called "process thought" would probably not see their system as a response to the failure of Bultmannianism, I think it can be argued that the popularity of their proposals can be measured in inverse proportion to the growing disillusionment with Bultmann's approach. To be sure, the initial outlines of process thinking precede Bultmann in time. Whereas Bultmann's work extended from the 1930s into the 1960s, Alfred North Whitehead laid down the foundations of what has become process thought in the earlier years of the twentieth century.[11] However, it has remained to the successors of Bultmann in America in the latter twentieth century to pick up Whitehead's thoughts, which had largely lain fallow for fifty or sixty years, and to develop them more fully.[12]

In many ways existentialism was a revolt against the dominant idealism that had ruled European thought throughout much of the nineteenth century. Most closely associated with the work of G. W. F. Hegel, idealism suggested that all existence was interrelated and progressing inevitably upward as the ruling principle of life, Divine Mind, unfolded itself in the process. The First World War called all that into question, and existentialism was one response. Writing and thinking during the first third of the twentieth century, Whitehead was still influenced by idealism but yet was seeking a way beyond it, and it is probably this feature of his thought that has made him appealing to a generation of American Christian thinkers who are questioning whether existentialism — Bultmann's or any other — really provides a way forward. As it stands, Whitehead's ideas seem to provide a place for history, that is, real human-historical experience in time and space, a place for a Deity who is involved in this human-historical experience, and a place for both progress and purpose in that experience — none of which, as we have seen, seem to be provided for in existentialism.

---

11. See especially Alfred North Whitehead, *Process and Reality* (London: Macmillan, 1929).

12. Two of the more prominent of these thinkers are John B. Cobb Jr. and Schubert M. Ogden. Another important figure was Norman Pittenger. For a recent treatment see R. Gnuse, *The Old Testament and Process Theology* (St. Louis, MO: Chalice, 2000).

A Description of Process Thought

The development of Whitehead's thought in recent times may be outlined as follows. God is actualizing himself in the process of history; that is, as history develops, so does God. In this sense God is both the source and the goal of all things; he began the process and he is that to which the whole process is moving. However, it is important to recognize that he is not other than the process. To think in those terms is to remove him from his active engagement in the process. Thus, there is a strong antipathy in this thought to what I have called above "genuine transcendence." Norman Pittenger goes so far as to say that a God who was not a part of the historical process could play no part in it.[13]

As a result of this insistence on the continuity between God and the historical process, there can be no plan or strategy for the unfolding of history. That would imply someone or something outside of the process defining it and evaluating its progress. No, all that we can say is that the unfolding is an expression of the compulsion to love. By "compulsion to love," it is meant that the divine in history is compelled to achieve its own self-realization, and that realization is achieved in creative self-giving. In that the divine and the world interpenetrate each other, the world moves to the same goal. How much this view of the goal of existence seems to be a reflection of biblical theology and how much is analogy from human relations appears to vary from writer to writer, depending on their own predilections.

Critique of Process Thought

Positive elements. From a certain perspective, there are several things about these proposals that make them attractive. For one thing, process thought sees God as being intimately involved with human life on every level. He is not restricted to "inner-personal" encounter but is directly engaged in every activity on the planet.

---

13. N. Pittenger, *Christian Faith and the Question of History* (Philadelphia: Fortress, 1973), esp. 124 – 25. Whitehead's concept of the dipolarity of God permits Pittenger to say, "[God] is also transcendent, but not in the deistic sense. His transcendence is found in that he is both free in and also unexhausted by his immanent activity" (117). By this he means that "God and the world are interpenetrating but distinct from one another" (116). This is not the biblical understanding of transcendence wherein God penetrates the world at every point, but the world does *not* penetrate God.

Second, because God is not a puppeteer, standing outside and pulling the strings, as it were, there is room for real freedom and responsibility. God is not making us choose this way or that, but when we do choose, God is as much affected by the outcome as we are. If we make a gain for the preeminence of love, God is enhanced, and if we fail and choose empty selfishness, God suffers and is diminished. *That* is responsibility. At the same time, this is not the radically lonely freedom of the existentialist, who chooses from a random list of options, knowing that in the end none of them really matter, but that he or she must still pay whatever unknown price those choices might entail.

Furthermore, process thought supplies at least a possible comprehensive answer to the problem of evil. Evil is not a "something," an entity; it is merely a negative, a violation of the compulsion of love. Thus, God does not cause evil; in fact, when it occurs he suffers more deeply than any of us. Yet at the same time his suffering is our suffering, because he and we are all inherent in the historical process.

Finally, this way of thinking makes history real and important, avoiding that bifurcation between fact and meaning that is such a troublesome aspect of Bultmannian thought.

Defects. But in spite of all these positive contributions, it must still be apparent that process thought has not solved the problem of biblical history, or if it has solved it, it has done so by doing serious damage to biblical thought. Above everything else is the issue of transcendence. If Bultmann removes God from the world, process identifies him with the world; and as I have tried to show at length above, all of the distinctly biblical ideas flow from genuine transcendence, from the idea that God is truly other than his creation. Whenever that principle is surrendered, the "other" worldview with all of its concomitant ideas flows into the vacuum. Whatever else process thought does it identifies God with the system. Here truly is "history myth" in place of nature myth.[14] History becomes the vehicle to explain God and God is identical to the vehicle.

---

14. So Pittenger (ibid., 64) says, "All entities belong together, for they are all participant in an interpenetrative and interrelational situation. Identity is found in the *continuity* of such relationships" (italics mine).

Thus, we are not surprised to find that there is no room for a personal God in this thought. Indeed, the "God" we find here is close to "the Force" of the *Star Wars* movies. While "the Force" has a generally "life-affirming" side, it is equally the locus of death and destruction and may well seduce persons in that direction. This is a slight advance over the myths in that there is here only one force that is given a mask of personification, but it is indeed only a slight advance.

Given the continuity between deity and the historical process, it is no surprise that no place is left for purpose in life. In non-Christian process thought God's self-actualization is not purposeful, and he himself (or it itself) does not know the goal of the process. Therefore, it becomes impossible to measure the progress that has occurred, or even more importantly, to *know whether progress has occurred at all.* In European idealism, the progress was obvious (or so it seemed). Europeans were better educated than others, better housed than others, more gainfully employed than others, and so on. That was clearly progress from the cave to the skies. Or was it? Process thought is a good deal less self-confident that it knows what the goal is or whether we are getting there. But that begins to sound a great deal as though the process is indeed not a progress at all, but merely an endless cycle.

Without clear purpose, there is no standard of evaluation. Thus, like continuity thinking everywhere, there is in process thought a disturbing tendency to baptize what is. Indeed, if the process is the actualization of God, then everything that occurs is part of the actualization. It may be responded that this is the glory of God, that he can take what seems to be evil and make it good. Yet what *is* evil, and what *is* good? If there is no Creator who made the world on purpose, who is to say that something is truly evil? If the serial killer gets genuine fulfillment out of his murders, who can say that is wrong? We are not *in* the image of God, we *are* the image of God, and God is being actualized in the entire process. Christian process thought seeks to make "self-giving love" as we see it in Jesus a standard of evaluation, yet apart from the Bible with its thoroughgoing transcendence, where does that standard get its authority? Hardly in the historical process as we have seen it unfolding in the last 150 years!

Finally, then, just as I question whether "love" can be sustained as a standard apart from the Bible and its insistence that God is *not* the historical process, I question whether we can talk about "development" of any sort apart from the unique biblical perspective. Does "the historical process" teach us about development or progress? Certainly we can look back over the past ten millennia and see certain signs of increased technical competence. We have moved from hunter-gatherers using sharpened stones as tools to bureaucrats communicating around the world electronically in seconds.

But is that progress? Or is it merely change? What is the goal toward which human society is tending? Or are we too, like our 10,000-year-old forbears, only wishing to survive as long as possible with a maximum of comfort, pleasure, and security? In fact, the idea of progress is dependent on the idea that our Creator has a goal for us, *outside of ourselves*, toward which we humans were made to progress and against which our progress can be measured. Give up that truth, and "progress" becomes a chimera.

Thus, while there is much about process thought that makes it more apparently compatible with biblical thought than is true of existentialism, we must conclude that it is a false hope. By rooting biblical theology in the historical process rather than in the unique events (and interpretations of those events) where the Bible roots that teaching, process thought has actually transformed biblical teaching into a near copy of the thought that the biblical writers fought against incessantly from Sumer to Rome and from 2000 BC to AD 100.

CONCLUDING OBSERVATIONS

What shall we conclude, then, in answer to the question with which we opened this chapter? Is it possible to "save" the theology of the Bible while denying the historical witness to the experiences that supposedly produced that theology? The answer to the question is "no." There is an internal logic out of which the theology grows, a premise on which it is based that is as essential to it as the conclusion. The apostle Paul states the logic in a terse and pungent way:

> If there is no resurrection of the dead, then Christ has not been raised; and if Christ has not been raised, then our proclamation has been in vain and your faith has been in vain. We are even found to

be misrepresenting God, because we testified of God that he raised Christ — whom he did not raise if it is true that the dead are not raised. For if the dead are not raised, then Christ has not been raised. If Christ has not been raised, your faith is futile and you are still in your sins. (1 Cor. 15:13 – 17 NRSV)

What is the theology? It is that human sin can be forgiven, our consequent alienation from God be repaired, and we can have eternal life with him. Where in the world did we get such an idea? Paul says we got it from the historic fact of the resurrection and the divinely given interpretation of that event. The resurrection proves that Jesus is God and that his death for sin could therefore be efficacious for all humanity. Furthermore, it proves that the physical death that is the temporal result of sin need not lead to an eternal dying of the body, but indeed can be reversed as the Spirit of the Resurrected One living in us gives life to the mortal body. Can that theology be successfully separated from the physical resurrection of Christ? Surely it would seem necessary since we know from *Historie* that humans do not rise from the dead! Obviously, Paul will have none of it. The theology is an interpretation of the historic event and apart from the historic event, the theology is simply illusory. One may believe one is forgiven and has eternal life and it is as vain as a delusion that one is Napoleon.

I maintain that Paul was not an innovator here. Rather, he is simply stating the logic of the Bible from end to end, using one example. What is that logic? We know God, and we know reality, because God has broken into our time and space and has revealed himself to us in that context. If in fact that "proclamation" (to use Paul's word) is based in falsehood, then not only do the Israelites not know God, they are found to be lying about him. But if that is so, how can we explain the remarkable ideas they have about him? That is the subject of the next chapter.

CHAPTER 9

ORIGINS OF THE BIBLICAL WORLDVIEW: ALTERNATIVES

As I have said above, Old Testament studies have undergone a remarkable shift in the last fifty years. We have gone from arguing that the unique features of the Old Testament must presuppose revelation in some form to denying that there are any unique features since we know that revelation is an impossibility. Nothing has changed in the biblical statements that earlier scholars found so radically different from those of Israel's neighbors. Rather, it is the conclusion that the biblical ideas *must* have evolved from the ancient Near Eastern ones, which then means that whatever appears to be the case, the biblical ideas *cannot* be essentially different but *must* be essentially the same with only superficial differences. I have argued above that indeed Israel's understanding of reality is at heart essentially different and that the only satisfactory explanation is the one the Bible gives: Yahweh's direct involvement in Israel's experience on a variety of different levels and a divinely inspired interpretation of the meaning of that involvement.

But I may not hold to that position without engaging recent attempts to account for the biblical understandings in ways that are very different from what the Bible says. If those explanations are convincing, then two things will be incumbent upon us. First, we shall have to explain why the biblical writers were at such pains to create other explanations for the origins of their ideas than the actual ones, and second, we will have to reexamine the claims to biblical uniqueness. If, however, those explanations cannot give a reasonable accounting for the biblical ideas, we are left at the starting gate asking, "If Israel says they got the ideas in this way, and there is no other reasonable explanation for them, should we not take Israel seriously?"

At the outset, I want to insist that we not rule out the possibility of divine revelation a priori. If we do that, then we have foreclosed the discussion. We have already presumed that Israel's theology is wrong, that if there is a God, he is inherent in the cosmos and is incapable of speech, that he is to be found in speculation upon the cosmos, and the like. That is, we have accepted in advance the thing the Bible says is not so. So we must begin by allowing the possibility that God is not the cosmos and that, therefore, if he is to communicate with us, it must be by direct revelation, indeed, by speech. We may conclude that this concept is wrong and that the Bible is mistaken, but if we begin by ruling out of the court the possibility of the biblical claims being correct, there is no discussion left.

I have chosen to review the arguments of four scholars whom I hold to be representative of different, but overlapping arguments on the point. All four, though to differing degrees, hold that the biblical explanation for its worldview, particularly as this is dependent on a certain perspective on Israel's history, is incorrect. The four scholars are John Van Seters, Frank Cross, William Dever, and Mark Smith. I recognize that to try to represent the thought of these prolific writers adequately and respond to them in such a short compass is to risk misrepresenting them, and in fact, even if unintentionally, be guilty of a "straw man" argument. If I do so, I can only say that I have sincerely attempted to guard against this.

John Van Seters: Israel's Understanding of Reality Arose as a Late Creative Fiction

I will begin with the arguments of John Van Seters. Professor Van Seters, in a series of ground-breaking books in the 1970s and 1980s, set the Documentary Hypothesis on a new path.[1] Up until that time, the arrangement and sequence of the documents lying behind the Pentateuch proposed by

---

1. See his *Abraham in History and Tradition* (New Haven, CT: Yale Univ. Press, 1975); *In Search of History: Historiography in the Ancient World and the Origins of Biblical History* (New Haven, CT: Yale Univ. Press, 1983). Subsequent works have included *Prologue to History: The Yahwist as Historian in Genesis* (Louisville: Westminster John Knox, 1992), and *The Life of Moses: The Yahwist as Historian in Exodus – Numbers* (Louisville: Westminster John Knox, 1994).

Wellhausen had largely reigned supreme. The earliest document was the J document from Judah about 900 BC, followed by the E document from Israel about 800 BC. These were synthesized into a narrative history of early Israel not long after the fall of the northern kingdom, roughly 700 BC. Over against these, Deuteronomy, the D document, emerged in 621 BC when it was planted in the temple to be found during the Josianic renovations. This was added to the JE document during and immediately after the Babylonian exile.

But after the exile, a new priestly party gained the ascendancy, and when their P document was merged with JED sometime after 400 BC, the normative understanding of Israel and its traditions was in place. Left by itself, the Documentary Hypothesis called for a fairly extensive rewriting of Israelite history and culture from that to be found in the Bible. But when form criticism with its emphasis on a long oral prehistory for traditional materials was overlaid on this scheme, it appeared that Israel's emergence and development, if not precisely what appears on the surface of Israel's documents, were not too much unlike the biblical picture.

But this picture still leaves too many unanswered questions if divine revelation is ruled out as a source for the Bible. How is one to explain the historical narratives of the Bible having long existed in oral form and then being written down several hundred years before anything remotely comparable in Thucydides and Herodotus? In response Van Seters proposed that in fact there was little of a genuinely historical nature in the JE "history," and that actually the bulk of that material was a "historical novel" created as a work of genius by an unknown person whom we must call "the Yahwist" in the sixth century BC. In other words, Israel's "history" grew out of the same instincts as those that account for the works of Thucydides and Herodotus and at roughly the same time. If it is less factually based than Thucydides, it shares something of the universalistic aims of Herodotus. If Herodotus sought to create a world history, the Yahwist sought to create a national history with the same sort of sweep. Thus, it appears that Van Seters has succeeded in showing that the Israelite national history is not unique either in its time or its aims.

As might be expected, having challenged favorite positions of almost everyone in Old Testament studies from one end of the spectrum to the other, Van Seters' work has been more of a catalyst for discussion than it has been generally accepted. One of the positive results that it stimulated, if not directly caused, was a renewed effort to see the Pentateuch as a whole. A notable work in this regard is R. N. Whybray's *The Making of the Pentateuch*.[2] Taking full account of Van Seters' work, Whybray goes even farther than Van Seters in arguing that the entire Pentateuch is the work of a single sixth-century BC historian who drew on Israelite folklore of a fairly recent vintage. Along the way Whybray rather trenchantly points out the weaknesses of both source and form criticism.

Perhaps the most pointed critique of Van Seters in a brief span is to be found in Frank Cross's *From Epic to Canon*, a compilation of articles by Cross revised for inclusion in that volume.[3] He asserts that Van Seters has ignored "the evidence of the linguistic typology of grammar and lexicon" and "sets aside all evidence of the oral background of much of the Yahwist and the oral origin of the archaic poetry of the Pentateuch." Furthermore, according to Cross, Van Seters has refused to take seriously "typologies of prosodic forms and canons [the way written forms developed in the ancient world] … of orthography, of narrative genres." He is also guilty of dating materials by means of the latest references found in the documents, when it is quite possible that these are only the result of "late editorial updating, or even an explicating gloss."[4] In short, Cross argues that there is much more evidence for the antiquity of the historical material in the Pentateuch than Van Seters is willing to grant. In particular, Van Seters' denial of the likelihood of lengthy oral transmission behind the written text of the Pentateuch is a sore point for Cross.

All in all, the argument that Israel's historical interests can be explained as arising "naturally" out of the same soil from which Thucydides and Herodotus arose must be seen, as Cross says, as "unconvincing." Once again, when these documents are read alongside the biblical accounts, it is

---

2. R. N. Whybray, *The Making of the Pentateuch: A Methodological Study* (Journal for the Study of the Old Testament Supplement 53; Sheffield: Sheffield Academic Press, 1987).

3. Frank Moore Cross, *From Epic to Canon: History and Literature in Ancient Israel* (Baltimore: Johns Hopkins Univ. Press, 1998).

4. All of the preceding quotations are from ibid., 29 – 30, n. 20.

not the similarities but the differences between the documents as wholes that strike one. In particular, the point of evaluation in the covenant as the expressed will of God is unparalleled. Whybray argues that Herodotus is just as much guided by "religious" concerns as is the Pentateuch, but it is just that the Greek religion is different from Israel's.[5] But that is just the point. Whence comes that difference?

And this point is complicated further if one grants, as both Van Seters and Whybray do, that the "Deuteronomistic Historian(s)" (those supposedly responsible for Joshua, Judges, Samuel, and Kings) were working somewhat in advance of the Yahwist. Whence comes for them the worldview that inhabits all their work? In other words, it seems to me that the "Achilles' heel" in both Van Seters' and Whybray's works is their inability to explain what it was about the experience of the exile that prompted a wholesale revisioning of the entire Israelite experience that was in such strong contrast to the pagan understanding that had supposedly preceded it.

FRANK CROSS: ISRAEL'S UNDERSTANDING AROSE IN A PROSE REWRITING OF AN EARLIER EPIC POEM

A part of Frank Cross's critique of Van Seters' position is necessitated by his own position, which is much different. Cross argued that the prose accounts of the Pentateuch (and of parts of the Former Prophets) are the result of a rewriting of a poetic epic much like the works of Homer into a prose form. He believed that this "epic was the creation of the league and had a special function in the cultus of its pilgrim shrines."[6]

In support of this thesis he points to Russian and Spanish examples where there has been an apparent move in the same direction from poetic epic to prose chronicles. He is careful to point out that these examples are not given by way of proof but merely as evidence that such a thing can happen. He also argues that there is every reason to believe that the courts of David and Solomon were able to produce a written work like that of the Yahwist (contra Van Seters and others).

---

5. Whybray, *The Making of the Pentateuch*, 229.
6. Cross, *From Epic to Canon*, 32.

In some ways this point of view is welcome, particularly when Cross asserts that there is good reason to believe that the old epic whose roots stretch far back beyond 1200 BC was able to faithfully preserve many of the elements of ancient institutions and lore. Yet in the end, in its attempt to provide a strictly human explanation for the distinctive view of reality that produced the distinctive Israelite literature, the proposal falls short.[7] The problem is that in spite of the Russian and Spanish examples, we have no examples of this shift having been made in Israel's own time and place. We have nothing comparable to Homer's poetic epic in the Bible, and we have nothing comparable to Israel's historical accounts in tenth-century-BC Greece. For the proposed analogy to work, we need to see Greeks turning Homer into history, and we need to have extant at least some of the Hebrew epic (Exodus 15 is not enough) that resulted in Genesis through Numbers. So the supposed analogy needs four feet to stand on but has only two, and they are not the same two in the two different cultures. The Greeks have only the epic, and the Hebrews have only the historical accounts.

Furthermore, the idea that "the league" preserved this epic in its cultic shrines is increasingly problematic. Martin Noth's arguments for something like the Greek "amphictyonic league" have been shown from several different points of view to lack solid grounds for comparison. Furthermore, Van Seters has argued convincingly that it cannot be shown that the historical narratives of the Pentateuch were ever connected with "a shrine."[8] So not only is the evidence for the existence of this epic thin, so also is the proposed method of its propagation and preservation. Moreover, there seems no sufficient cause for its translation into a narrative history unparalleled elsewhere in the ancient world.[9] So again, I do not believe that Cross's explanation is adequate to explain where the biblical ideas came from.

But perhaps both Cross and Van Seters have been looking in the wrong place for the origins of Israelite thought. Perhaps instead of looking at literary issues, we should be looking much more in the direction of the history

---

7. Whybray, *The Making of the Pentateuch*, 163, attributing the proposal to Albright, says "it has very little to support it, and has generally been rejected."

8. John Van Seters, *Abraham in History and Tradition*, 139–48.

9. It does not seem to me that the Solomonic empire needed the Genesis accounts or the Exodus-Numbers narratives to validate its existence.

of religions, and in particular at Canaanite religion. Is it not possible that Israelite religion is in fact only one more of the West Semitic religions and that Yahweh is only a mutation of Chemosh, Baal, and Hadad, to name three? Two persons who have garnered a good deal of attention on this front are William Dever and Mark Smith. While their professional interests have been somewhat different, with Smith focusing more on texts and Dever more on archaeology, both have come to somewhat similar conclusions, though Dever's most recent expression of it is more polemical. Mark Smith has written three books in recent years, all with rather provocative titles, and all address the question of the emergence of Israel's religious views.[10] William Dever has also authored three recent books.[11]

WILLIAM DEVER: ISRAEL'S UNDERSTANDING IS AN IMPOSITION OF A SMALL ELITE

One can discern a certain trajectory in Dever's three books. In *What Did the Biblical Writers Know and When Did They Know It?* he lays out the overall picture of his thought, which is then expanded upon and developed in the two later volumes. Dever is an archaeologist of Palestine (he was one of the first to deplore the expression "biblical archaeology"), trained at Harvard University under G. Ernest Wright, and he is particularly concerned to recover the history of biblical times in the light of archaeology.

Dever finds himself at odds with persons on both ends of the spectrum as regards what we can know about ancient Israel. Although early in his career he began to question the "Albright synthesis," which gave a fairly high level of historical veracity to Israel's traditions, he now finds himself unable to go to the extremes of the so-called "minimalists," whom he calls "nihilists." These persons (among whom are Philip Davies, Thomas Thompson,

---

10. Mark Smith, *The Early History of God* (San Francisco: Harper and Row, 1990); *The Origins of Biblical Monotheism: Israel's Polytheistic Background and the Ugaritic Texts* (Oxford: Oxford Univ. Press, 2001); *The Memoirs of God: History, Memory, and the Experience of the Divine in Ancient Israel* (Minneapolis: Augsburg Fortress, 2004).

11. William Dever, *What Did the Biblical Writers Know and When Did They Know It?* (Grand Rapids: Eerdmans, 2001); *Who Were the Early Israelites and Where Did They Come From?* (Grand Rapids: Eerdmans, 2003); *Did God Have A Wife? Archaeology and Folk Religion in Ancient Israel* (Grand Rapids: Eerdmans, 2005).

and Keith Whitelam) have all proposed, in one way or another, that Israel as the Bible depicts it never existed. Dever argues directly and forcefully that there is good (in his terms, irrefutable) archaeological evidence confirming the existence of Israel as a people during the first millennium BC.

At the same time, Dever with equal fervor denies on the basis of archaeology that much of what the Bible depicts as the religious history of Israel ever occurred. Leaving aside the patriarchs, he asserts that there is *no* evidence to believe that there was an exodus (although one might question exactly what that evidence would consist of). From that point he moves on to deny any evidence to support the biblical picture of a massive conquest that is pictured in Joshua. He finds the portrayal of Israel's situation that is found in Judges to be much more compatible with his understanding of the data.[12] From this point on he argues that the data do support the existence of a state of Israel, and then of the two states, Judah and Israel.

But in all of this, Dever argues increasingly strongly against the Bible's religious (or spiritual) explanation of Israel's existence and nature. He says, "We now know … that the 'official' portrait in the Bible is highly idealistic, reflecting largely the view of the elite, orthodox, nationalistic sects and parties that produced the versions of the traditions that we happen to have in the Bible."[13] So the diatribes of the prophets are not against people for diverging from what they had previously committed themselves to; rather, they try to coerce the people to leave what they had always worshiped and to move to the worship of this austere new god whom the prophets were in the process of creating.

This thesis is expressed most forcefully in the third of the three books cited above: *Did God Have a Wife?* He argues that Israel's dominant religion was indistinguishable from ordinary Canaanite religion until after the exile and that there is clear evidence for this in the Bible. The reason

---

12. One wonders if this is not to play Joshua and Judges against each other too completely. If Joshua is read carefully, it does not describe a war of occupation (note the continual return to the base at Gilgal), but rather one that breaks the control structure of city-state confederations, leaving the people free to then occupy the land in small segments, as Judges describes. See K. Kitchen, *On the Reliability of the Old Testament* (Grand Rapids: Eerdmans, 2003), 159–95 on this point.

13. Dever, *What Did the Biblical Writers Know?* 270.

this evidence has been ignored, he says, is that the white, Western, male, Christian Protestants who have dominated biblical studies have only been interested in "biblical theology," an enterprise he seems to consider spurious. He goes on to say that because he is a former fundamentalist Christian and now a nonpracticing Jew, he can approach the subject in a more unbiased way.[14]

That can hardly be the case. The evidence is open to a number of different interpretations, as the work of interpreters as different as Richard Hess and Mark Smith indicates. Each of them, Hess more exhaustively, reviews the evidence for widespread worship of the goddess Asherah in Israel and comes to the conclusion that it is not there.[15] Is it not possible that Dever's reading of the evidence is the result of bias? He states his position and his argument most concisely in chapter 8 of Did God Have a Wife? titled "From Polytheism to Monotheism." In brief, he argues that the point of Exodus 6:3 is that "Yahweh" was indeed an imposition on the earlier El cult, which was fully pagan. It was just that the imposition came much later than the Bible now maintains. It was the work of a tiny urban elite (less than one percent) sponsored by the state bureaucrats of Judah, and was brought to expression in the propagandistic "histories" of the group, which were ultimately formalized into the "Deuteronomic history."

All this time the mass of the people were fully devoted to the old religion, which was especially focused on Asherah, the "mothering" goddess. The kings, like Hezekiah, seeing an opportunity in the emerging Yahwism, sought to use it to force greater unity on the common people, who still preferred their ancient, diverse folk religion. When the exile came, it must have seemed to deal a devastating blow to all the forms of folk religions that apparently failed so disastrously. Thus, the small, fanatical Yahwist elite was well positioned to hammer home its points against its demoralized opponents. So they emerged from the exile as the only contestants still standing and in the return (for which they fabricated "previous predictions" in the prophets) they proceeded to sweep away the last vestiges of opposition.

---

14. Dever, Did God Have a Wife? 88 – 89.
15. Richard S. Hess, Israelite Religions: An Archeological and Biblical Survey (Grand Rapids: Baker, 2007), 350; Smith, The Early History of God, 125 – 33.

I cannot respond to all the ramifications of this proposal in the limited space here. But I simply want to ask if it is a sufficient explanation for the particularities of the Bible as they now stand? It seems to me that a series of at least four questions remains unanswered. First, if the biblical account is such a dramatic rewriting of the facts, why did not the "historians" do a better job? If they truly wanted to make it appear that Yahweh had been worshiped exclusively in Israel from the ancient past, why did they leave in the supposed evidence that this is not so? Why did they not, in creating their national story, simply remove all evidence of Israel's pagan tendencies?

Dever responds by saying that it turns out that they were better historians than we thought. But that will not do. If they do not hesitate to change the reality enough to project Yahweh far back into the past, why would they care about being "honest" enough to leave in the record some data that does not serve their purpose, especially when they warp it? If they are writing propaganda, as Dever repeatedly insists, any concern for accuracy, especially since it is not genuine accuracy in his view, goes by the boards.

A second question arises from this same point. Where does the interest in "historical" reporting come from in this scheme? I have argued that it comes from Israel's unique experience with Yahweh. But if there was no such experience, and if Israel's religious experience was, in fact, identical to that of every other people in the region, where does the desire come from to write one's religious convictions in terms of the choices and responsibilities of humans in relation to the revealed will of the one God? Dever says that some things will have to remain a mystery, because archaeology cannot answer everything. That is not a sufficient answer.

The third question has to do with the idea of a state-sponsored religion. How can state sponsorship explain the clear capacity of Israel's religious documents (and prophets) to stand in stark judgment of the monarchy? Dever says that since it was a Judahite undertaking, of course all the northern kings are accused of apostasy. But so are all but five of the Judean kings (including the greatest Judean king of all, Solomon). Where does that come from, unless from a tradition, or an understanding, or a Person, who stands outside of the state and the royal house?

My fourth question has to do with the heart of the matter. Where in Dever's process did thinkers in Israel shift from continuity to transcendence, and what in his process accounts for the shift? Was it in the exile, which biblical scholars increasingly seem to want to make the stimulus for all Israel's religious insights? That will not do. Unless that fanatical elite had already come to that understanding, the book they supposedly brought from exile with them, which had such a devastating impact on the poor pagans back home, could not have been created in that time. But without the insights of transcendence, the documents that they took with them *into* exile could not have existed, because the particular shape, content, and outlook of those books can only be explained by transcendence. Or did the concept just dawn on some erstwhile pagan scribe somewhere in the Solomonic chancellery some quiet afternoon and slowly filter into the thinking of the other one percent of Israel's urban males? The unique combination of transcendent personhood that now provides the sole foundation of biblical thought never emerged anywhere else in the mind of a scribe or a philosopher. Why did it emerge in a thoroughly pagan Israel?

MARK SMITH: ISRAEL'S UNDERSTANDING IS A NATURAL DEVELOPMENT FROM WEST SEMITIC RELIGION

Mark Smith, to his credit, has given the most thought to these questions. In the books cited in note 10, he argues at great length for the origins of Israel's faith in Canaanite polytheism. He is at pains to locate any references in the Bible that could point to such origins. I have referred to most of these in the chapters above and have argued that the references need not be taken in those ways, that in virtually every case there is another explanation for the materials that if not actually better, is at least equally plausible.

But my interest here is not with those arguments, but with where Smith goes from his conclusion. He notes that in its present form the Bible is remarkably monolithic, preserving much less of its origins than one might think. Thus, as noted above, he is quite candid in saying that little evidence remains in the Bible in support of a living Asherah cult in Israel.[16] But if this is true, if the religion of Israel down into the early monarchy was

---

16. But note more willingness to entertain the idea in his *The Memoirs of God*, 64.

indistinguishable from the religion that flourished at Ugarit three or four centuries earlier, and yet the Bible is so different from that, how are we to envision the process from the one to the other?

Although not all of his suggestions and explanations appear in Smith's latest book, *The Memoirs of God*, it comes the nearest to offering a full explanation of the process. Here he argues that the biblical understanding is a result of the challenges that Israel faced in its existence, both politically and environmentally. For example, the monarchy was a response to such a challenge when the loose-knit tribal structure of the Judges period was unable to stand up to the threat of the technologically superior Philistines. The social critiques of Amos and Hosea were prompted by the challenge posed by the rise of a small wealthy class that was taking over the family lands of a previously more egalitarian people. During this time, down to about the eighth century BC, Yahweh was slowly emerging as the dominant god, and Smith thinks that there were two impetuses for this, both arising from Israel's situation.

One was the emphasis on family, so that Yahweh came to be seen as *pater familias* (i.e., the benevolent but dominating head of the family around whom everything circled); the second was the emergence of the monarchy and his being defined as king. These two together began to move him to a dominant position. But it was the challenge of the fall of the northern kingdom that galvanized those responsible for Deuteronomy to think in terms of oneness: one God with one law worshiped in one place. Now Yahweh is King and no other, including the earthly king. When the greatest challenge of all — the exile and the return — faced Israel, the ancient traditions about a landless people led by one Lord to their true home were recast in such a way as to make hope possible.[17]

To all of this, I must ask, did no one else in Tyre, or Syria, or Amon, or Moab, or Edom face such challenges? The answer is that of course they did — many of them precisely the same challenges. Yet, none of them produced anything even faintly resembling the Bible and its worldview. And

---

17. It is remarkable to me that in his examination of the challenges Israel faced and the way in which he believes their faith emerged from the crucible (ibid., 46 – 85), Smith seems to give their purported covenant with Yahweh no attention at all.

did none of those other peoples move from a tribal-family-oriented situation into having a king? Again, they all did. Yet, not one of them ever suggested, let alone made it a way of understanding all reality, that there is but one God, who is so much not to be identified with his world that he cannot be represented in any created form. Smith replies that we do not know enough of the cultural situation of the neighboring countries to be able to answer the question.[18] I do not think that is a satisfactory reply.

Smith suggests a way in which the pantheon of Ugarit could have developed into the Israelite understanding of deity. He notes that the deities at Ugarit were arranged in four levels.[19] They are as follows:

1. El and Asherah, the king and queen of the pantheon
2. Baal and Astarte/Anat, the prince and princess, but also Mot, the god of death, and others such as Shamash (the sun) and Yerah (the moon)
3. Kothar, the magician and court counselor
4. The rest of the gods — messengers and servants

He then supposes that a similar situation applied in early Israel, with the exception that on the second level, along with Baal and Astarte/Anat, there were the gods Shahar, Shallim, Resheph, Debir,[20] and the intruder Yahweh from somewhere south of the Dead Sea. It is also interesting that the name of the Israelite magician/counselor on the third level is unknown since later writers so thoroughly expunged it.[21]

The supposed second stage in Israel (early monarchy?) looked like this:

1. El and Asherah, plus Yahweh, who has insinuated himself into this position
2. Depersonalized natural elements such as the storm, the sun, moon, and stars

---

18. Ibid., 121.
19. This seems to have been generally true of all the pantheons in the ancient Near East.
20. These are names that appear in the Old Testament. Whether they were ever considered gods in Israel is unknown.
21. Or is it not equally likely that there never was a magician/counselor god in Israelite religion?

3. ?

4. Resheph, Debir, the angels

The proposed third stage (from the late monarchy) looks much the same as the second. But the fourth stage in the development is remarkably different:

1. Yahweh
2. Empty
3. Empty
4. The angels

Of course, of these four supposed stages in Israel's religious development, the only one we know from the Bible is the last, with stages one, two, and three being entirely conjectural on the basis of the slimmest of evidence from the biblical texts.[22] Furthermore, the jump from the hypothetical third stage to the fourth stage is simply too great. El's disappearance can be explained by Yahweh's usurping his roles, but how did Asherah become dethroned, and how did the sun, moon, and stars cease to be divine? In short, Smith's explanations for the way in which the Yahwism of the Bible arose simply have too many unanswered questions in them.

I do not flatter myself that I have dealt in any kind of a full way with the vast array of material that I have surveyed in these few previous pages. That was not my purpose. My purpose was to ask if current scholarship has been able to present a convincing explanation for the unique features of the biblical worldview and the ways in which that worldview affects the understanding of reality in the Bible. My conclusion is that it has not. It has not shown what mechanisms or procedures would have or could have resulted in *this one place* in an orderly evolution from the thought of continuity and its implications to the thought of transcendence and its implications. I can only conclude that the biblical explanation remains the best one.

---

22. Once more, if we are to think that these supposed pieces of evidence do point to a very different religious history than the text describes, then we have to say that the writers of the final form of the text did a poor job of correcting their sources.

CHAPTER 10

CONCLUSIONS

This work has centered on the observation that in comparison to the other literatures of the ancient Near East, the Bible is characterized by a worldview that is sharply different from all the rest. I have called the Bible's view *transcendence* and the other one *continuity*. In the first, the divine is other than the cosmos; in the second, the divine is inseparable from the cosmos. This difference is so significant that even today there are only three religions that believe in true transcendence: Judaism, Christianity, and Islam — and all of them have derived that conviction from one source only: the Bible.

This difference in worldview results in a sharp difference in the manner of representation of one's understandings of life. Whereas the Bible sees unique, nonrepeatable events and persons within time and space as being fundamentally important to knowing God, the other literatures do not. Instead, they represent what is important for understanding life as occurring either outside of time and space altogether, that is, in primeval time and space, or as in representative human figures whose space/time location is insignificant. In this regard, the other literatures clearly believe that it is in the retelling of the narratives about the gods that the order and productivity of the world is maintained. This understanding has been historically defined as *mythical*. Hence, we defined *myth*, following the lead of Brevard Childs, as a form of expression, whether literary or oral, whereby the continuities among the human, natural, and divine realms are expressed and actualized. By reinforcing these continuities it seeks to ensure the orderly functioning of both nature and human society.

Historians, anthropologists, sociologists, and others have all sought to understand where this mythical way of viewing reality has come from. Initially it was argued, and is still current in popular thought, that this was a "primitive" way of thinking, that people did not think "scientifically" because it was beyond their mental capacities at that point. Few in the academic community today hold to this view. It is one thing to describe *how* a people thought and quite another to explain *why* they thought that way. It is hard to look at the accomplishments of the Sumerians or the Egyptians in the third millennium BC, or for that matter, the Mayas in the first millennium AD, and say that these people were incapable of genuinely empirical thinking. They show every evidence of being able to analyze data logically and to arrive at testable conclusions. No, if they understood reality in that way, it was not because they were incapable of "more advanced" thinking.

A second possibility is that these societies had limited information.[1] Every society stands on the shoulders of those preceding it, so perhaps these early thinkers had not yet accumulated enough information about the world to realize that the forces of nature are not to be personified, or that the rules of logic that operate in the physical world must be applied to the spiritual world as well. Thus, it has been argued, the Greeks were the beneficiaries of all that went before them and they then arrived at true thought, which is pure speculation based on depersonalized data. But if that is the case, if the mythical worldview is simply the result of not knowing better, how are we to explain the fact that both Greece and Rome were again thoroughly wedded to myth five hundred years after Aristotle? And why, on the other side of the coin, did Greek scientific thinking reemerge a thousand years later and come to permeate the thought of Christian Europe?

If mythical thinking is not to be explained by primitive mentality or by limited information, is there a third possibility? Yes, there is, and that possibility is choice. People have chosen to think about the world and reality in these ways. Nor can they be blamed for having done so. If one begins with the premise that everything that is, is contained within this psycho-socio-physical cosmos — that is, in the words of British theologian Colin Gunton, "the world itself provides the reason why things are as they are"[2] — then certain results will necessarily follow. This is especially true

---

1. So John Rogerson, *Myth in Old Testament Interpretation* (Beihefte zum alttestamentliche Wissenschaft 134; Berlin: DeGruyter , 1974), 182 – 83.

2. Colin Gunton, *The Triune Creator: A Historical and Systematic Study* (Grand Rapids: Eerdmans, 1998), 36.

if one concludes that an exclusively materialist explanation of things is not able to account for all the data.

One hundred years ago the philosophy of Auguste Comte, called positivism, was popular. In it Comte argued for a completely materialist understanding of reality. There *is* no spiritual world. In that context, it was laughable to maintain that there is a spiritual component to reality that one ignores at his or her own peril. So Arthur Conan Doyle, creator of Sherlock Holmes, made himself ludicrous by his credulous writing on spiritualism. But, interestingly, fewer persons are laughing now. An America naively confident of its ability to master the material world and produce a fully satisfying life finds itself in the position of the child who has seized a soap bubble and asks, "Where did it go?" And so we have begun to wonder if there is not more to this self-contained cosmos than we thought.

To all this, the ancient Sumerians would say knowingly, "We thought you would get here sooner or later." Thus, the issue becomes one of finding ways to understand and control this immaterial element. Ultimately, the only way of understanding is by analogy to this sensuous world we know, and the only means of control is through the assumption of correspondence or continuity. Thus, Thomas Molnar speaks of "the pagan temptation" in his book of the same title.[3] He shows how again and again this way of thinking has insinuated itself into Western thought from the neo-Platonists to the present. His depiction of the neopaganism of the present is only more poignant now twenty years after he first wrote it.

Nor when we speak of neopaganism are we permitted to imagine it as a group of dreadfully serious people dressed up in funny robes muttering dark imprecations while dancing in a circle around a fire on which smolders a chicken. To be sure, this way of thinking may take that expression, but it is by no means limited to such an expression nor even best represented by it. It is a serious concern to so imagine the spirit component of the world as to come into communion with it and gain its benefits for oneself.

Why has this happened? Not only is it the result of the failure of our materialism to bring any lasting satisfaction, but on a deeper level, it is the result of the failure of the Enlightenment experiment. If ordinary people

---

3. Thomas Molnar, *The Pagan Temptation* (Grand Rapids: Eerdmans, 1987).

believed that material well-being would bring satisfaction and fulfillment (i.e., happiness), the intelligentsia were certain that it was rational objectivity (i.e., science) that would lead us to the pinnacle of human perfection. Now it has become painfully obvious that science is only able to answer life's secondary questions — the "how" questions — but is an abysmal failure in answering the primary questions — the "why" questions.

Comte could say that there were no metaphysical questions, but we, to our sorrow, know better. We are faced with the real possibility of unlimited technical virtuosity in the control of beings utterly without virtue. This would be the ultimate dis-order, and we feel that we must find ways of reaffirming and retaining order, at least for our own fragile lives. Rational objectivity, we think, is responsible for this intellectual and moral bankruptcy. It has created a world that is heartless and feelingless, devoid of mystery, and powerless to produce what it promises.

The forerunners of this rejection of the Enlightenment were seen in the "revolution" of the 1960s. One of the "cult books" of that period was the narrative account of the research findings of a UCLA doctoral candidate named Carlos Casteneda.[4] For his research purposes he apprenticed himself to a Yaqui sorcerer in Arizona. The sorcerer used various hallucinogenic drugs to produce altered states of consciousness in which the participant could gain power in and over the spirit world.

At the same time, more learned works promoting the validity of the mythical understanding were appearing. One of the more prolific writers was Mircea Eliade, whose early experimentation with yoga had a profound effect on him.[5] It appears that one of Eliade's concerns was to understand

---

4. Carlos Casteneda, *The Teaching of Don Juan: The Yaqui Way of Knowledge* (New York: Washington Square, 1968). Based upon the popularity of *Don Juan* Casteneda produced five more books about the sorcerer. It was later shown that the entire series, including the first upon which his doctoral dissertation was based, was fiction. I think this is not accidental. After all, what is "history" in a world of continuity? There are no grounds for calling one thing "true" and another "false." "True" is true for me.

5. On this point see Guilford Dudley, *Religion on Trial: Mircea Eliade and His Critics* (Philadelphia: Temple Univ. Press, 1977), 114, 117. Some of Eliade's more important books are *Patterns in Comparative Religion* (London: Sheed and Ward, 1958); *The Sacred and the Profane: The Nature of Religion* (London: Harcourt, Brace, Jovanovich, 1959); *Myths, Dreams and Mysteries: The Encounter between Contemporary Faiths and Archaic Realities*

myth in such overarching terms as to make it the defining character of religion of any sort. Thus he defined myth as a means of remembering, of reorienting oneself with the originating event or events. In this regard historiography is a form of myth, and to tell the gospel story is to participate in the myth. In the same way novel writing is a form of myth-making because in it the writer and the reader are seeking to escape the bonds of particular time.

All of this recalls the discussion of the definition of myth above in which it was seen that the definitions have become so broad as to be useless for the purpose of classification. If historiography is a form of myth-making, then is not myth-making history writing? And we have then descended to the level of incommunicability where all things mean everything and nothing means anything. But of course that is exactly where continuity thinking tends. To communicate we must be able to *distinguish* between one thing and another, whereas in a world of continuity, all things are at bottom the same.

Another expression of continuity thinking in the present time is to be found in the thought and work of C. G. Jung. In his book *The Empty Self: Gnostic Foundations of Modern Identity*, Jeffrey Satinover, who describes himself as a former Jungian practitioner, details some of the ways in which Jungianism presumes an understanding of reality that is fully in keeping with the tenets of continuity thought.[6] Of course foundational to all of this is the concept on which modern psychiatry is built, which most moderns (and postmoderns) accept as a given: that all of us are conditioned by pre-existing immaterial forces so that none of us is finally free or completely responsible. But as Satinover makes plain, Jungianism went well beyond that with its ideas of the collective unconscious in which we all partake, with the concept of the archetypes to which all of our thinking conforms in one way or another, and with his understanding of dreams as the door to another reality than the illusory world of time and space in which we are presently trapped. Once again, the ancient Sumerians would have preferred

---

(London: Harvill, 1961); *Myth and Reality* (New York: Harper and Row, 1963); *The Two and the One* (Chicago: Univ. of Chicago Press, 1965).

6. Jeffrey Satinover, *The Empty Self: The Gnostic Foundations of Modern Identity* (Wheaton, IL: Hamewith Books, 1995).

more concrete language to communicate all of this, but they would have been perfectly at home with the ideas.

Finally, and most explicitly, we have the work of Joseph Campbell, which received considerable impetus from public television in the six-part series moderated by Bill Moyers, entitled *The Power of Myth*.[7] Campbell insisted that all symbols the world over finally point to the same realities that stand outside of the visible world. But the symbols do more than point to the realities. Finally, the symbols are indistinguishable from the realities. To engage in the symbolic activity is to engage the reality.

For Campbell, the great sin of biblical religion is in its exclusivity, in its insistence that its symbols are the only acceptable ones. The biblical concept of transcendence, that the Deity is utterly other than the cosmos, is profoundly wrong. There is a transcendent realm, namely, the invisible world, but to suggest that it is beyond the cosmos is to render it meaningless to us. The only workable worldview is the worldview of continuity. So Robert A. Segal, his biographer and interpreter, writes: "From [his] first work to last the true meaning of myth is a-historical rather than historical and symbolic rather than literal ... myth preaches the oneness of at once consciousness with unconsciousness and the everyday world with the strange, new one."[8]

The examples cited above, from Castaneda to Campbell, all underline the point that the worldview of continuity is neither the result of "primitive mentality" nor limited information, but of choice, whether conscious or unconscious. Thus, we should not think, as I tried to show in the previous chapter, that the biblical view of transcendence would have evolved from continuity as some sort of a logical next step. That idea is a carryover from the world of nineteenth-century idealism, in which there was seen a steady progression upward from animism to the highest form of religion: ethical monotheism (which just so happened to correspond to the religion of

---

7. Some of Campbell's more important works are: *The Hero with a Thousand Faces*, 2nd ed. (Bollingen Series 17; Princeton: Princeton Univ. Press, 1968); *The Masks of God*, vols. 1–4 (New York; Viking, 1959–1968); *The Power of Myth*, with Bill Moyers, ed. B. S. Flowers (New York: Doubleday, 1988).

8. Robert A. Segal, *Joseph Campbell: An Introduction*, rev. ed. (New York: Penguin, 1990), 265.

nineteenth-century Europe). These two views, transcendence and continuity, are in direct contradiction with each other and are mutually exclusive; neither is able to exist in the presence of the other.

In the end, as Molnar showed, transcendence is too painful. To embrace it is to give up control of the universe. It is to admit that the only thing I can do to get in line with whatever is in control and to "get on its good side" is to surrender in trust, belief, and obedience. It is to confess that I cannot with my own intelligence ferret out the meaning and significance of life. It is to admit the other side of what Gunton called an "inescapable" choice: that "God ... provides the reason why things are as they are."[9] It is to refuse the serpent's suggestion that I can not only become *like* God, I can actually *become* God. This is a frightening place to live, and the other understanding is much more comfortable.

So, in view of world history, what may we expect if we take the road down which Eliade, Jung, Campbell, and a host of others are pointing? It seems to me the outcomes are clear, and several of them are already to be seen.

1. First and foremost, ethics as an internal compass will disappear from among us. Ethics will certainly remain as civic desiderata, and there will be various public attempts to enforce them, but in the society at large they will be meaningless.

2. "Truth" will progressively be replaced by power, since there is no standard of reliability outside of each person's own needs and wishes.

3. "Right" and "wrong" will become increasingly useless terms as they lose any agreed-upon basis outside of those same wants and needs. The terms will continue to be used, but only as code words for those who can shout the loudest.

4. There will be a dramatic upsurge in interest in "black magic" as a means of getting one's way.

5. Any attempt to control absolute sexual freedom in any area and at any level will be labeled as "hate-mongering."

6. Individuals will be increasingly devalued at the same time that "individual freedom" is more and more loudly trumpeted.

---

9. Gunton, *The Triune Creator*, 36.

7. Altruism and other forms of self-denial for the good of others will steadily disappear.
8. Acceptance of responsibility for one's own behavior, accompanied by appropriate changes of behavior, will be a rarity.
9. The study of history, except as an arcane antiquarian interest, will disappear.
10. The possibility of a genuine transformation of one's character from the worse to the better will be dismissed out of hand.[10]

Do I make these predictions as a member of some "right-wing religious hate group," whose adherents are opposed to the modern world? Not at all. I make them as a professional student of ancient Near Eastern history and religion and as an amateur student of the religions of the world. These features, in one form or another, are the common characteristics of those cultures where continuity thinking has prevailed. Thus, if we in the West turn away from that explanation of reality that has only the one fountainhead, the Bible, to the only other alternative understanding of reality, we should not be at all surprised to reap that understanding's historic results.

What shall we say then? Are there striking similarities between the Bible and the religion it describes and the ancient Near Eastern literatures and the religions found therein? There certainly are, and we should be surprised to find it otherwise. Israel is described in the Bible as a full participant in its world. But what we find is that those similarities are not the defining features of the Bible or of biblical religion. This is unmistakably evident to anyone who takes the Bible as a whole. I refer to my earlier illustration: if one simply lists the component parts of a dog alongside those of a man, one might conclude that they are essentially the same. But if one takes "dog" as a whole and "man" as a whole, what can one conclude but that they are *in their essences* different? So also, if we look at the Bible as a whole, where else is there anything like it in its world, or indeed, in *the* world? There is nothing like it. In its historical narratives covering the sweep of a nation's existence *and* the glories and tragedies of individual life, it is unparalleled.

---

10. On these themes, see George Weigel, *The Cube and the Cathedral: Europe, America, and Politics without God* (New York: Basic Books, 2005).

Beyond that, where else is human-historical experience the arena, and the only arena, where God is to be known? Its law, built on ancient Near Eastern law, is transformed by incorporating it into a covenant with Israel's Creator encompassing all of life. Its prophets, sharing with Israel's neighbors the idea of receiving a word from God, are incomparable in their making the future dependent on present human moral and ethical choices growing out of covenant obligations. Its liturgical practices, nearly identical with those of its neighbors, are shaken down to the ground by the insistence that in and of themselves those practices accomplish nothing. Its wisdom literature, sharing many of the same concerns and even expressions of wisdom literature elsewhere, nonetheless stands alone in making wisdom a moral and spiritual matter expressive of one's relationship to God. Finally, in their views of the origins of the world, one need only read the biblical accounts alongside any other to be impressed that in spite of superficial similarities of expression, the two pieces are in every other way different.

How are we to account for these essential differences? All of them find their rootage in one single revolutionary concept: the Creator of the universe is radically other than his creation. Thus, Yahweh is not a part of his environment and cannot be manipulated through it. Moreover, he cannot be finally understood by reflection on the environment. Further still, his will and being are not bound up in the cyclic functioning of the environment. But neither is it possible for us as creatures to function on his level. Thus, it becomes necessary for the Transcendent One, if he wishes to be known — and he does — to "translate" himself into our "language." But if he is personal, and ethical, and consistent, and loving, all of which he is, that "language" cannot be the cyclic existence of an impersonal natural environment. Instead, the "language" will have to be that of the human-historical environment. As the one Creator of the universe, with no rival, he is not only in a position to judge us if we fail to live up to the purposes for which he created us, he is also able to redeem us from those failures, if he should choose to do so.

So how shall we account for this unique understanding of reality? Should we not give credence to the explanation that the Bible gives of itself? If it alone, of all previous and subsequent thought about reality, presents an Ultimate who is both truly transcendent and fully personal, should we not credit its own explanation? Shall we say that the Hebrews, just like all their neighbors, took this cosmos as the given and then imagined the invisible part of the cosmos through an analogy with the visible part and alone arrived at a different understanding of reality than *everyone* else who followed that method? Beyond that, shall we say that those Hebrew thinkers, explicitly denying their actual method, then laboriously created a complex but almost entirely fictional explanation of the origins of their thought? Does that not strain credulity too far, unless, that is, we have decided a priori that the biblical explanation is impossible?

The Bible, essentially different from all other religious literature (except that derived from it), claims to be the result of God's breaking in upon distinct persons and a distinct nation in unique, nonrepeatable acts and words. It is now a revelation of God to us because not only are the actions and messages recorded by divine inspiration, but so also are the interpretations, and the transmission of this material has been divinely superintended so that the resulting Word is fully capable of being used by the Holy Spirit to produce the same affect and effect in us as did the original acts and words. If we do not grant this possibility, the one the Bible claims, we are left with no satisfactory explanation for the biblical worldview and theology.

In the end, we may differ on the questions above and the answers we give to them, but what matters in the end is how we answer the following questions: Is there a God? Does he have a will for our lives? Has he made known that will to us in intelligible actions and speech in time and space? If we answer any of these with "no," then the entire enterprise is bootless. We are simply playing with the pieces of a mental puzzle on our way into the dark. How we put the pieces together is of little importance. If, however, our answers are "yes," the question of what God's will is and how he has chosen to reveal it becomes one of absolutely ultimate significance.

SUBJECT INDEX

Author Index

We want to hear from you. Please send your comments about this book to us in care of zreview@zondervan.com. Thank you.